Lest We Forget

THE HISTORY OF THE FRENCH IN KERN COUNTY

by

Mary Grace Paquette

Holder of a Ph. D. degree in French literature from the University of California, Santa Barbara, Professor Paquette is chair of the Department of Foreign Languages at California State College, Bakersfield.

A publication of the
Kern County Historical Society
and the County of Kern
through its Museum

1978

PIONEER PUBLISHING CO.
FRESNO, CALIFORNIA

*Copyright © 1978
by the Kern County Historical Society
All rights reserved
Manufactured in the United States of America
Pioneer Publishing Co.
Fresno, California 93728
ISBN 0-914330-14-4*

to my French friends

CONTENTS

		Page
Foreword		ix
Preface		xi
Chapter		
I	French Argonauts On The Kern	1
II	The French Colony In Kern	15
III	French Stockmen In Kern	25
IV	Along The Sheep Trails	45
V	Havilah: A Mining Town	53
VI	Bakersfield: The Emerging San Joaquin	57
VII	French Settlers Of North Kern	71
VIII	East Bakersfield: Heart Of The French Colony	95
IX	Tehachapi: Little Béarn	135
X	The French In The Oil Era	143
Epilogue		151
Appendix	Selected French Place Names In And Around Kern County	152
Bibliography		154
Index		157

FOREWORD

By the 1970s Kern County's once flourishing French colony had virtually ceased to exist, and only a few "old timers" could recall its heyday. It was timely, therefore, that Dr. Mary G. Paquette and students in her classes at California State College, Bakersfield, a dedicated group of researchers, began a study of this ethnic group in order to preserve at least its historical identity.

While engaged in their research Dr. Paquette and her students interviewed some seventy "old timers," recording their recollections on tape. Documents were studied in San Francisco, Sonora, Mariposa, Kern, and Los Angeles Counties. Historical materials—books, manuscripts, and newspapers—in the libraries of the principal towns of these counties were read. In this way the researchers gained an understanding of the role of the French miners, sheepmen, ranchers, and businessmen, as well as the social life of the colony.

Once the research had been completed Dr. Paquette, with care and understanding, wrote the history of Kern County's French colony. It is a privilege for the Kern County Historical Society to be able to publish this unique ethnic study. Hopefully this French project will inspire other ethnic groups to take steps to preserve their historical identities in Kern County.

W. Harland Boyd

PREFACE

"There used to be a lot of Frenchmens around here, but they're all gone now." So went the typical wistful response to early queries made when a projected history of the French in Kern County was first under way.

Many people seemed unaware of the existence of any sort of a French colony in Kern County, or they tended to confuse the French and the Basques. However, the histories of these two peoples are dissimilar enough to justify first the story of the "Frenchmens," as they refer to themselves, and to reserve the story of the Basques for another study. After all, the French generally preceded their Basque counterparts in settling the southern end of the San Joaquin Valley and were, in fact, among the first Europeans, after the Spanish, to set foot in Kern.

It is a somewhat arbitrary decision to confine this study to the French in Kern County, however. To begin with, there were French in this area long before there actually was a Kern County. The French settled throughout the state with the major concentrations to be found in San Francisco, Los Angeles, and along the rivers of the interior. The colony in Kern was actually a branch of the greater colony which even today has its head in San Francisco. And there was at all times a great amount of mobility, of families moving from one area of concentration to another. The French have always been clannish, which helps explain why almost always they are found clustered together. Each area, nonetheless, has made its own imprint on the people who have settled there, and so it is with the French in Kern.

As early as 1832, French fur trappers under the leadership of Michel Laframboise were already combing the canyons and crannies of the San Joaquin Valley in search of the once plentiful beaver. Early writings reveal that the Hudson Bay Company continued to send its employees into the valley until approximately 1845. However, the chief rendezvous for the French Canadian trappers was located north of Kern County at a place called French Camp, four miles south of Stockton. One can only speculate that their numbers included the quasi-legendary Pierre Lebec or Peter Lebeck, as his name was carved on the tree which marked his grave near Fort Tejon.

The first French to arrive in any substantial numbers and actually settle in Kern County were the gold miners. Gold was discovered along the Kern River in the early 1850s, and the French quickly spread out from their diggings on the Feather River or "Plume" as they called it to seek the elusive yellow metal farther south.

French immigration to Kern began, then, as a trickle in the 1850s and gradually increased to a veritable torrent in the seventies and beyond the turn of the century. Even as gold was becoming scarce, its dimming luster still lured a second generation of Frenchmen to these parts. They flocked, men and women alike, to all corners of the county but in particular to what is today East Bakersfield, believing the reports from their friends and relatives that the streets were literally paved with gold. Awaiting their chance to strike it rich, the men generally became sheepherders, an occupation which provided them with the opportunity to walk over almost every square inch of valley floor and mountain slope, their eyes watchful for the slightest glimmering speck beneath their feet. Most found no gold but instead made, lost, and a few even made again, a fortune in the production of wool.

The sheepmen formed the kernel of what was known as the French Colony in Kern. Life was hard but they took comfort in their numbers. It seems as though almost everyone was related in one way or another. The heyday of the colony ran from the turn of the century until the outbreak of World War I. During that "Belle Epoque," life centered around the hotels where many a marriage was made over those better than home-cooked meals which cost only twenty-five cents including wine.

But the war was to change all that. French immigration to Kern, although never ceasing entirely, dwindled to practically nothing as more than a million French lives were lost in the holocaust on their home soil. Many of the local sheepmen were forced to take their families back to France to reclaim and carry on the patrimony. By the late 1920s, most of the French who remained here were no longer herding sheep in Kern County, nor were they clustered together in East Bakersfield. Of those who elected to stay, some settled on ranches and turned to farming, but most took city jobs. As sheepherders the French were already being replaced by the Basques, and their businesses and homes in the heart of the old colony were frequently taken over by Italians.

Nevertheless, French interest in Kern County resurged briefly in the first decades of this century when the oil boom was in full swing. There were two French-owned oil companies with interests in and around Bakersfield, whose presence caused a temporary influx of Frenchmen to the area.

And so the history of the French in Kern unfolds in a triptych-like pattern. It encompasses the gold, sheep, and finally the oil eras. While these eras overlap one another chronologically, it is the middle one, the sheep era, which is of the greatest significance. For it was then that there was truly speaking a French colony in Kern. The men and women who brought their dreams from so far away have made a permanent place for themselves in the history of the area.

May we never forget them and the heritage they have left us.

I am grateful to all who have helped to bring this project to fruition. While I cannot acknowledge everyone personally, I must mention some non-French friends who gave generously of their time and talents. I thank W. Harland Boyd for the many hours spent reading my manuscript and also for sharing his vast knowledge of Kern County and its inhabitants with me; Richard Bailey for providing me with special resources from the Kern County Museum; Jack Clare and Alan Grupe for their insights into the Ardizzi-Olcese era; Cecil Dyar, my Delano expert; Herb and Ola Mae Force, my Tehachapi historians; Nina Caspari, my library friend; Guy Doolittle, J. L. Guy, and Bernard Turpin, for corresponding and talking to me about the oil era in Bakersfield; Sue Glenn and Diana Mushaney, for typing my manuscript; and especially my Senior Seminar students at California State College, Bakersfield, for being, on so many occasions, my eyes and feet.

CHAPTER I

French Argonauts On The Kern

Prior to the discovery of gold at Sutter's Mill early in 1848, there probably were only a handful of Frenchmen in the Mexican province that became the State of California. Once the gold excitement was underway, Frenchmen joined the rush of wealth seekers who came from all parts of the world. By 1851, although they were outnumbered by the Germans, there were an estimated 20,000 Frenchmen in the state. Mostly they were working in the northern mines, and they were especially active along the Feather River. An exact count of them was impossible because the term "French" encompassed all who spoke the language, including the French Canadians. They were lumped together as the "Keskydees," a corruption of the phrase meaning "what is he saying?"

When the news of the discovery of gold in California reached Europe, emigration companies were formed in France and these launched publicity campaigns intended to encourage Frenchmen to join the gold rush. Actually no great effort was needed to encourage them to leave their homeland. At that time the country was suffering the throes of economic difficulties, civil strife, and revolutionary activities. The resulting repercussions were widespread, but they especially affected the outlying provinces of France.

Although the French émigrés succeeded in escaping the problems at home, they began to experience new kinds of difficulties in the mines of California. American miners quickly made it known that they resented the competition of foreigners in the search for gold. The fledgling state legislature was pressured into imposing a tax of twenty dollars a month on each foreign-born miner. Subsequently the tax was removed after vociferous complaints, especially from the Mexicans and Frenchmen working the San Joaquin River. Understandably some of the Frenchmen anglicized their names in the hope of avoiding discrimination. Who could guess that Bob Wettel, owner of the Barbarossa Mine in Kern County, was in fact a Frenchman from Paris who had been naturalized in Kern County? County documents relating to the granting of citizenship and registration to vote reveal that many others anglicized their names. Among those individuals who changed their names, but admitted to birth in France, were Charles B. Lewis, a Kernville shoemaker, naturalized at New Orleans, and John K. Smith, a Caliente laborer, naturalized in Calaveras County.

Frenchmen were among the thousands of gold seekers who in the spring of 1855 joined the short-lived rush to the Kern River, in the southern Sierra Nevada. In spite of some initial discrimination against them and the realization that the mines were not bonanzas, many remained in the mines to comprise the "fifty fabled Frenchmen" of the Kern River diggings. Some of them, according to a report reaching the San Francisco *Alta California* during the gold excitement, were "taking out large quantities of the metal." The same newspaper early in 1859 reported that the French miners were still enjoying success, and that they were working "with... zeal and vigor." Later in that same year a correspondent of the Visalia *Tulare County Record* characterized them as "peculiarly fortunate." This success he attributed to "their energy," and he observed that they worked harder than the Americans.

Outstanding among the French gold seekers in the Kern River mines was Jean B. Chevalier, referred to respectfully as Monsieur Chevalier. Reportedly he knew more about extracting gold from quartz rock than anyone in the district. Under his "magic wand," according to a report reaching the San Francisco *Alta California* early in 1859, quartz mining was about to make a "fresh start." Late in 1861 another French miner, Dr. Claude de la Borde, was characterized by the Visalia *Delta* as one of the oldest and most persevering miners in the district."

French Argonauts On The Kern

Customarily the French miners listed their claims with the secretaries of the various mining districts, and the names of some of them are to be found in the surviving documents. Late in 1857 a claim was filed for the French Doctor's Mine in Greenhorn Gulch by, among others, Jean Boisseau, Théophile Drago, Jean B. Couvreur, and Claude de la Borde. Frenchmen working other mines in the gulch were Serre Borgas, Charles Legrain, and Emile Lorrette.

Named for miner Richard Keyes, Keyesville, a small settlement near the confluence of the North and South Forks of the Kern River, was the principal trading center in the Kern River mines. Near the crest of the nearby Greenhorn Mountains there was another smaller settlement called Petersburg. Its leading merchant for several years was Eugène Caillaud who had come to San Francisco during the gold rush to California. Within a few years he had reached the Greenhorn Mountains where he was involved in both storekeeping and mining. The Eugene Grade, on the climbing road between Little Poso Flat and the crest of the Greenhorn Mountains, was named for him. After many years of mining activity, Caillaud was killed in 1886 by a caving gravel bank, which it was rumored was not an accident.

In the early 1860s mining activity spread upriver from Keyesville, which led to the founding of Kernville on the right bank of the North Fork of the Kern River. The organizers of the adjacent mining district specifically denied "either by location or purchase" claims by Negroes or Chinese, but they made no such mention of the French. Frenchmen worked the mines of the district, but apparently few established businesses in the thriving settlement.

On the other hand, Dr. Claude de la Borde, familiarly known as the "French Doctor,"* was in the vanguard of the prospectors who launched mining activity in the mountains south of Keyesville. With Benjamin T. Mitchell, Alexander Reid, George McKay, Hugh McKeadney, and Asbury Harpending, among

---

* A pattern emerges as the first of a type is distinguished by the adjunct "French," as in the French Doctor, the French Ranch, and the French Hotel.

others, he found gold in the vicinity of Clear Creek in mid-1864. Within a few months a booming town named Havilah had been founded in the district, and the prosperity surrounding it led to the creation of Kern County in mid-1866. The new town was designated the county seat. Havilah soon acquired a sizeable French population, including some of the town's leading businessmen.

With his partner Auguste Gouglat, Claude de la Borde laid claim to the Dijon, Rhône, Rochefort, Navarre, Nièvre, Lyon, Marengo, and French Friend Mines in the Clear Creek district. The sale of these holdings in 1865 for $50,000 enabled the discoverers to return to France, as was reported by the Havilah *Courier*, "to enjoy a life of ease and plenty." Assertedly "no two men ever left a district more respected than these two gentlemen."

The New Eldorado mining district, at the eastern base of the Piute Mountains, was formed in the mid-1860s during a flourish of mining activity. One of the best mines in the district was the St. John, which was discovered by Félix S. de St. Jean, a French Canadian. In that district also were Edward Beaudry and John Farran, who likewise were from Canada. In 1868 St. Jean acquired a part interest in the stage company that operated between Havilah and Los Angeles.

Other French miners were active in the Tehachapi Valley, at the juncture of the Sierra Nevada and Tehachapi Mountains. There mining continued until the placers became unprofitable and the high water table made it impractical to deepen the mine shafts. By the 1880s most of the French miners had left the valley, and at least some of them turned to ranching and farming in Kern County. Among the identifiable French miners who were active in the Tehachapi Valley but who became settlers were Jean Pierre Bizac, Charles Henri Doriot, Pierre Lestelle, and Victor Ponsard.

Countless other Frenchmen because they were not citizens and were without the right to vote nor owned property left virtually no official or legal evidence of their presence in Kern County. Yet how widespread was their mining activity is indicated by those who became citizens and registered to vote.

French Argonauts On The Kern

Listing themselves as miners were, among others, Julien A. Baillif of Caliente, Etienne Chabraie of Long Tom, Constant Hourdé of Woody, and Georges Weydenecht of Piute.

When the mines east of the Sierra Nevada were booming in the 1870s, a French Canadian was the leading freight hauler on the bullion road between the Owens Valley and Los Angeles. He was the well-known Rémi Nadeau, proprietor of the Cerro Gordo Freighting Company, whose business interests occasionally brought him to Bakersfield and Caliente in the San Joaquin Valley. Late in 1875 he offered a reward of fifty dollars to anyone who could prove that barrels of liquor were being tapped or cases opened by employees of the freighting firm. A private detective, Frank Drake, discovered that one of the culprits was Edward Oriot, a Frenchman who kept the Indian Wells Station. He had formed a lucrative partnership with a teamster, Francisco Villega, alias Spanish Frank. The teamster had been removing goods from his wagons and passing them along to the stationmaster who in turn sold them. When arrested Oriot posted a $4,000 bond and fled, only to be retaken by the intrepid detective who found him with fellow Frenchmen at Darwin. Oriot then was placed in the Kern County jail at Bakersfield.

Nadeau had amassed a considerable fortune through the successes of his freighting business, and this enabled him to launch other business ventures in the late 1870s. Boldly he paid $20,000 for a small adobe grocery store owned by Auguste Bouelle at the corner of First and Spring Streets in Los Angeles. There he built the town's first four-story structure, which was opened as the Hotel Nadeau in 1884. Four years later Nadeau died at the age of sixty-eight.

Long after the Kern River mining excitement had subsided Frenchmen like Virgile Bernard, Martin Martin, and Jean Robert continued to work sporadically the Big Blue Mine near Kernville and the Comet Mine high in the Greenhorn Mountains. The hard-working Frenchmen who came to the Kern River mines hoped to "strike it rich," and the hillsides scarred by the miners' picks and blasting powder are their enduring monuments. The fortunate ones departed with the wealth they wanted, while the less fortunate turned to other enterprises, went to newer mining districts, or returned to France. By the 1870s another wave of Frenchmen was beginning to reach Kern County, and many of them engaged in sheep raising, a pastoral pursuit that afforded an occupation for a host of emigrating Frenchmen.

Ancelle, the village in the Champsaur Valley which probably sent the most Alpine French to Kern County. (Photo courtesy of Odile Zampa Giordano)

Léon and Bernard Bimat and wives Malvina and Marie (Rostain) with their father Edward Bimat and Bernard's daughter Marie. The Béarnais Bimat brothers married two sisters from Dauphiné. (Photo courtesy of Alice Bimat)

Lest We Forget

Kern City's most popular bridesmaid, Marcelle Philipp, with Léa Grimaud, the bride of Joseph Espitallier. (Photo courtesy of Dolly Espitallier Ansolabehere)

The Clerou family and relatives in Oloron Ste. Marie. Front row: Romain Lesot, Marie Clerou, Lucy (Ferran) Clerou, Jean Lesot, Grandmother Félina Ferran, Louis Lesot, Uncle Jean. Second row standing: Marie Lesot, Louis Clerou, Jean Lesot. Back row: Jacques Ferran, Léon Ferran. (Photo courtesy of Vincent Clerou)

Marie Etchebarne of Saint Etienne de Baigorry met her future husband, Justin Chevalier, while working as a maid at Marius Plantier's French House. (Photo courtesy of Helen Chevalier Banducci)

Justin Chevalier, born in La Plaine in the Hautes Alpes in 1867, came to Kern in 1887 to join his older brothers. (Photo courtesy of Helen Chevalier Banducci)

Lest We Forget

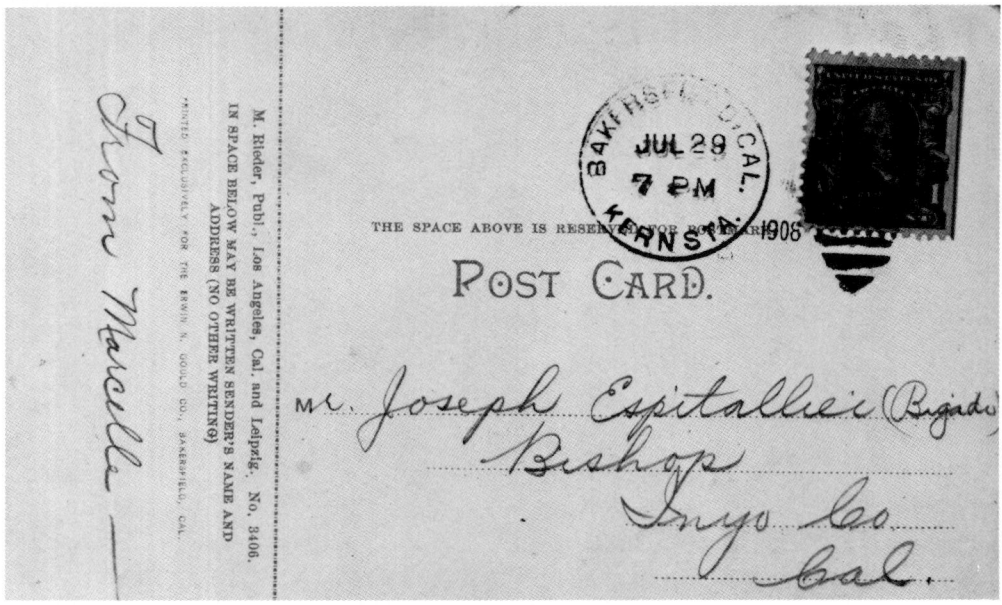

A postcard mailed by Marcelle Philipp on July 29, 1908 to Joseph Espitallier, which uses the sobriquet "Bigado" to identify the proper recipient. (Postcard courtesy of Louise Espitallier Kuhs)

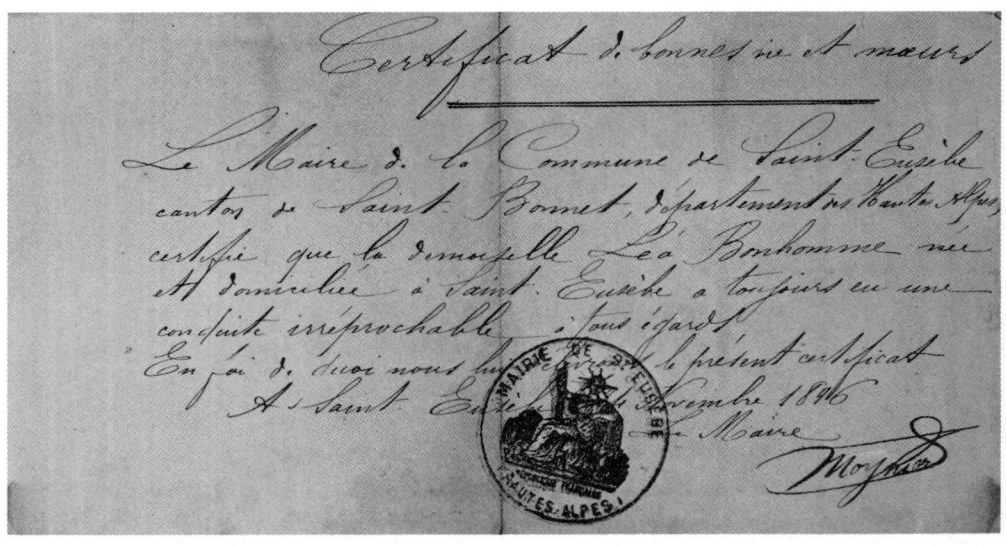

Certificate of good conduct for Léa Bonhomme, signed by the mayor of St. Eusèbe, November 24, 1896. (Document courtesy of Winifred Barthélemy Sasia)

French Argonauts On The Kern

A Béarnaise, Marie (Cazanave) Raymond, and a Dauphinoise, Lucille (Pellisson) Espitallier.

The 1914 Bastille Day float with Queen Alice Borel.

The 1918 Bastille Day float with Queen Marie Roux. To her left: Eloi Michel. At back corner of float: Henri Espitallier. To far right of picture: Jules Delagne, holding flag, and Eli Eyraud.

Draft notice for Elie Matheron, dated December 10, 1883. (Document courtesy of Armanda Gueydan Bosley)

Léon Abonel with the Amourig Stables on East 19th Street as a backdrop, circa 1911. (Photo courtesy of Leah Provensal Castro)

Auguste Martin, ready to serve under the American flag in France, in 1917. (Photo courtesy of Auguste Martin)

August Villard, son of Ambroise and Eugénie (Faure) Villard, as a doughboy in 1919. (Photo courtesy of Anne Villard Blanc)

CHAPTER II

The French Colony In Kern

Many of the French settlers who came to Kern County, beginning in the 1870s, were the sons, daughters, nephews, and nieces of those who earlier had come to California stricken with gold fever. The favorable reports of those first comers were particularly well received in two fairly remote parts of the homeland. These were the Upper Alps (Hautes Alpes) and the Lower Pyrenees (Basses Pyrénées). Nestled in the Alps of southeastern France was the ancient province of Dauphiné, and at its heart was the Champsaur Valley. A few dozen families lived in each of a string of villages which, in spite of their small size, almost all contributed sons and daughters to the western part of the United States. Undoubtedly Ancelle was the most generous in sending pioneers to Kern County. Its counterpart in the province of Béarn, at the base of the Pyrenees near Spain, was Oloron Ste. Marie. Although the Béarnais who came to Kern County claimed it as their birthplace, in reality most of them were born in the outlying areas. Most of Kern County's French pioneers came from the Alps, however.

The willingness of Frenchmen to leave their homeland in the 1870s was understandable in light of the unstable economic and political conditions in France. With the fall of the Second Empire, following an unsuccessful military confrontation with Prussia, and the unsteady beginnings of the Third Republic, the country faced an uncertain future. Moreover in the Alps and Pyrenees the families tended to be large, while the natural resources were limited. Periodic disettes or famines plagued these mountain areas, where usually the oldest son remained to work the family farm, the youngest son cared for the aging parents, and the other children went in search of a better way of life, a quest that brought many of them to the United States.

In addition some French men left the homeland in order to avoid compulsory military service. Elie J. Matheron's draft notice, issued at Ancelle in 1883, noted that he had already departed for the United States. Listed on the document were the penalties imposed on an individual avoiding service, as well as the jeopardy of anyone aiding or abetting an evader. Having once left France, few evaders dared return to the native land. Later men over fifty-four years of age were allowed to return with impunity, but younger ones were imprisoned if they stayed longer than three months. In 1929 Eugène Eyraud, whose wife's family lived in Kern County, visited in France longer than he had intended because of the illness of a sister, and he was imprisoned for eighteen months.

French women emigrated for some of the same reasons that prompted the men to seek a new way of life in the United States. As members of large families during hard times, without a promising future, they succumbed to the glowing accounts of life abroad. With so many of the young men leaving home, it was perhaps inevitable that they would follow in their wake. Since there usually was a shortage of women in the sheep country, there was a steady demand for wives in the western part of the United States.

Many a tear was shed as the farewell scene was played time and time again at the mountain railroad stations in the Alps and Pyrenees. After obtaining the necessary papers, including certificates of good conduct from the mayors of their communes, the youthful emigrants went by train to Le Havre, and from there they sailed to New York. During the gold rush travelers had reached San Francisco by way of Cape Horn or the Isthmus of Panama, but after the completion of a transcontinental railroad in 1869 they boarded westbound excursion trains from New York. Some of the emigrants reached Los Angeles, but a greater number arrived at San Francisco, which had the larger French colony. After stays of varying lengths in these larger cities, most of them fanned out to the smaller colonies in the

The French Colony In Kern

western states. Ultimately several hundred of them settled in the southern San Joaquin Valley.

When they arrived in the United States few of the French émigrés spoke English or were familiar with the values of American money. In the fall of 1875 the Bakersfield *Southern Californian* reported the amusing anecdote of a Frenchman who had difficulty with the language. Someone obligingly had written out for him the present tense of the verb *to go* as follows: "I go, thou startest, he departs, we make tracks, you cut sticks, they absquatulate." In money matters some could only hold out a handful of unfamiliar coins and hope that an honest conductor or salesperson would take only what was needed. Occasionally newspapers carried stories of the disappearance of émigrés in the course of long journeys. At the final destination the newcomer was met by a compatriot, or he presented a letter asking that he be directed to a residence or, more commonly, to a French hotel.

Although French family names often bore a relationship to the part of France from which the bearer came,* numerous unrelated families shared the same name. Common among these were Espitallier, Escallier, and Eyraud. In order not to confuse persons of the same last name, the sobriquet commonly was used. These sometimes indicated the village of birth, as in the case of Jean "La Motte" Eyraud, while his brother Eli, because of his size, was known as "Colosse." "Long Valley" Joe Eyraud, who was not a relative, took the name of the area where he grazed his sheep. Auguste Lagier was called "By Thunder" because "by tunder," as he pronounced it, was his favorite Americanism. Little "Shakey Joe" Vial reputedly had a nervous condition that could only be quieted by a shot of liquor. An almost legendary sheepman by the name of Jean Pierre Escallier was known as "Quatorze" because he had served in the Fourteenth Battalion of the Chasseurs Alpins. More confusing yet were the cases of those persons having the same first and last names.

---

* The suffix "aud" is readily identified with the Alps and can be found in many French names associated with the Kern area: Jaussaud, Richaud, Grimaud, Eyraud, Rambaud, etc.

Among these computer-defying combinations were André André, Robert Robert, Martin Martin, and Philippe Philippe.

The majority of the French who emigrated to the United States severed virtually all ties with their native land and sought American citizenship. Typically they were reticent to discuss their backgrounds, not because they were ashamed of their ancestry, but because they were determined to be Americans. A few, after having attained a moderate degree of success and affluence, in their later years returned to France.

Because the French men were determined to wait until they were fairly well established economically before they married, a twenty year age difference between a French husband and wife was not uncommon. While many of the first arrivals never married, some found brides among the Mexican and Spanish women. But once the French women had become more plentiful, few married outside their nationality. A few returned to their native villages and found wives, but most of them accomplished the same purpose by visiting the French colonies in San Francisco and Los Angeles.

Starting especially in the 1890s a large number of the French men chose wives from among the hotel maids of East Bakersfield, and needless to say the hotels were always seeking new maids. Until the opening there of St. Joseph's Catholic Church early in the twentieth century, the marriage ceremonies were frequently performed in a hotel. While a Dauphinois generally married a Dauphinoise and a Béarnais a Béarnaise, there were a few inter-marriages. For example Léon and Bernard Bimat, brothers who were natives of the Pyrenees, married sisters Marie and Malvina Rostain, who were born in the Alps. Occasionally a Béarnais or Béarnaise married a Basque, but this was rarely the case with the Dauphinois or Dauphinoise. Yet, for example, Justin Chevalier, who was born in the Alps, married Marie Etchebarne, a native of Saint Etienne de Baigorry in the Pyrenees.

As the decades passed the American "melting pot" had an increasing influence on the second and third generation French families in Kern County. Ties with the European culture grad-

The French Colony In Kern

ually were obliterated, and there were a larger number of marriages with non-French partners. While unions of persons of French and Basque ancestry continued to be rare, there were frequent marriages between descendants of the Alpine French and the Piedmont Italians. More than was the case with the French of the Alps and the Pyrenees, these people shared an ancestral similarity of dialects and customs. Especially in Kern County were there unions between second-generation French daughters and Italian sons, among them marriages which united the Banducci-Chevalier, Lorenzi-Eyraud, Sasia-Barthélemy, Panero-Villard, Sandrini-Boisseranc, and Iacopetti-Boisseranc families.

When recalling life in a typical French menage in East Bakersfield, Ernestine Baker described the domestic routine in the home of her parents, Léon and Lydie Abonel. The conservative father, believing as he did that a wife's place was in the home, did all of the grocery shopping. Among other things this afforded her little chance to learn the English language. Ordinarily she prepared a breakfast of coffee, bread, and eggs for her husband, but if he was in a hurry she gave him two raw eggs in a glass of wine. Until midday she was busy preparing the noontime meal, which was the principal one for the family. This routine of domestic activity continued into the afternoon and evening. Most of the children of French parentage at first spoke the patois or dialect of the family, and only when they entered school did they learn the English language.

The French migration to Kern County reached its climax about the opening of the twentieth century, and then it dwindled to an insignificant number in the 1920s. At the climactic point there were almost daily arrivals from the Alps and the Pyrenees. The diversity and sheer number of articles in the local newspapers on life in France attest to the size and importance of the French colony. Scarcely was a newspaper issued in the 1880s and 1890s that did not include an article dealing with French culture, including a beautiful love poem in French that appeared in the spring of 1889.

Seemingly forgotten were the harsh anti-French sentiments of the 1870s. When the editor of the Bakersfield *Kern County Californian* in the fall of 1884 received a copy of a French language newspaper published in Los Angeles, he praised this endeavor to preserve French culture, describing it as "a large and well printed weekly journal." Although he was unable to comment on its "literary or other merits," he was "inclined to concede" that the French were "first class," and "especially in the walks of literature" they rarely did "things by halves."

For many decades, in good and bad times, Kern County's French colony observed the patriotic national holiday of the homeland, July 14, known to Americans as Bastille Day. A correspondent of the Bakersfield *Californian* in 1891, captured by the spirit of the merrymaking, paid homage to the French community in its own language. In translation it was reported that they had celebrated "an unforgettable date for the French people," one that marked "the beginnings of both French democracy and independence which, until then, had been suppressed under the yoke of monarchic despotism." Observed by all of the French residents of Bakersfield and the surrounding areas, "the celebration was characterized by a spirit" which only the French could "give to such an occasion." He was pleased to have such citizens as neighbors, and he joined with them in the hope for a long-lived independence.

A few days later a correspondent supplied the editor of the *Californian* with a fuller account of the festive day of celebration. Under the management of "chiefs of amusement" Jean Eyraud, Jacques Dusserre, Barin Relixto, and Alfonse Faure, a "magnifique" picnic and dance was held. "Altogether the picnic was a grand success," and the dancing continued until sundown. In the evening the celebrants enjoyed other social events in East Bakersfield, including a birthday dinner given by Eugène Verdier, whose natal day fell on Bastille Day. After dinner most of the guests "accepted the invitation to the dance" at the home of Jacques Dusserre and "enjoyed themselves until the musicians got weary." Doubtless these reported social events were only a few of those held on Bastille Day in 1891.

The carefree times of the early 1890s were overshadowed by

The French Colony In Kern

the unhappier ones in the years ahead, but the traditional Bastille Day celebrations were held, with a short wartime hiatus, until the 1920s. In between were the bad times of the mid-1890s and later the stormy outbreak of World War I. The Great War had a profound effect on all expatriated Frenchmen, including those living in Kern County. By then a grand parade with floats had become a part of the Bastille Day celebrations, and the floats of 1914 and 1918 reflected an obvious contrast in prewar and postwar feelings. In 1914 Queen Alice Borel was aboard a horse-drawn wagon surrounded by six white doves, the long-standing symbols of peace. Yet French military readiness was emphasized by a life-sized black eagle poised for flight, as well as by a threatening cannon manned by Joseph Vivian, who bore no casual resemblance to General Joseph J. C. Joffre, the commander-in-chief of the French army.

The older French pioneers were beyond the age for military service, but a few of the younger ones responded to the French appeal for men and returned to the homeland. On the other hand, American-born French men had the opportunity to go to France under the stars and stripes of the United States. While serving in France many of them visited the villages of their parents and met for the first time relatives eager for news about long-departed family members. Upon the resumption of the Bastille Day festivities in 1918 emphasis was on Franco-American cooperation. The contrasting symbols of peace and military strength were still in evidence, but Queen Marie Roux reigned over a float bearing the theme "United then - 1776, United now - 1918." Kern County's French colony was never quite the same as it had been in prewar years. France suffered more than any of the victorious countries from the holocaust which was fought largely on its soil. Nearly a million and a half soldiers and a half million civilians died in the conflict. In many instances the only surviving heirs to patrimonies lived in Kern County, and several families felt obliged to move back to France. The resulting small-scale French exodus helped speed the demise of the French colony in Kern County.

During the postwar years France made an all-out effort to

repair the ravages of the conflict, and there were few émigrés. As the years went by economic conditions in France, including the Alps, improved, making it less pressing to find a living elsewhere. In America Frenchmen were less interested in sheep raising, and in the western states often they were replaced by young Basques, who readily left their homes in the lofty Pyrenees.

The world-wide Spanish influenza epidemic which came in the wake of World War I took its toll in the French colony. Among the hastily written entries in the death records of St. Joseph's Church in East Bakersfield were many French names. Alongside of these were those of other nationalities, which fact afforded evidence of the growing cosmopolitan character of East Bakersfield. No longer the dominant foreign group in that community, the French were being joined by Basques, Mexicans, Italians, and Greeks.

Many of the French hotels were closed with the approach of Prohibition, and barrels of whiskey and wine were emptied into the gutters. Yet various French families continued to get together, taking turns, for the express purpose of making wine and beer in basements. After all, the stereotype of a Frenchman and his wine had to be preserved. Seemingly the authorities turned a blind eye to these vinicultural activities in East Bakersfield.

In the 1920s the Bastille Day festivities, including the picnics, attracted large crowds which were difficult to manage, and as a consequence these events were discontinued. Yet the French still clung together, and certain happy traditions persisted. After attending church on Sundays families continued to visit their friends, in the earlier days going by buggy but later by automobile. Among the pleasant summertime experiences, especially for the children, was a visit to a sheepherder's camp. At attractive locations old bachelor sheepherders provided neat tents for the visitors, and these hosts also did the cooking, baking, and roasting of lambs for their sustenance.

Early in the 1940s another generation of young men of French ancestry went off to war, and during World War II several, because of their linguistic backgrounds, served as interpreters

The French Colony In Kern

for the armed forces. Again some of them had the opportunity to visit friends and relatives in Europe, as had an earlier generation during World War I. Many families living in the Alps and the Pyrenees still speak of the "cousins from Bakersfield."

By the end of World War II little was left of the French colony anywhere in Kern County. Families which once had clustered together in distinct neighborhoods had drifted apart. Many of the homes in the French quarter of East Bakersfield were destroyed during the extension of Truxtun Avenue. Only a handful of the most recent wave of émigrés are alive today, and the children of the pioneers have become parents and grandparents. With the successive generations came a fading of the memories of the old French colony, and only dim traces of the French presence remain in the southern San Joaquin Valley.

CHAPTER III

French Stockmen In Kern

The primeval Coast Range, Tehachapi Mountains, and Sierra Nevada, as well as the enclosed southern San Joaquin Valley, comprised a vast pasture land. In this stockmen's paradise there was an abundance of public domain on which to graze cattle and sheep. With the disruption of the South's economy during the Civil War, there was a shortage of cotton in the United States. In California cattle raising declined in favor of sheep raising. By 1870, with wool ascendant as a textile, there were three million sheep in the state. Needless to say, the Kern County sheepmen played no small part in the developing sheep saga.

Among Kern County's pioneer ranchers were a comparatively large number of Frenchmen, some of whom were former miners, but most were newcomers from France. Unlike his brother Eugène Caillaud, a Parisian who came to America in search of gold and eventually reached the Greenhorn Mountains, Charles Caillaud came to the same locale and became a cattleman in the late 1860s. He predeceased his brother by eight years, but his plucky widow, Frances (Guillon), aided by her sons and sons-in-law, operated the ranch until her death in 1911. After brief ownership by a son-in-law, Auguste Pierre Eyraud, a Bakersfield businessman, the property was sold to non-French owners, but it continued to bear the name French Ranch. Another Frenchman, Hippolyte "Harry" Sarret, gave up mining and settled with his bride Juliette (Caillaud) at Poso Flat, on the northwest slope of the Greenhorn Mountains. From his ranch he sent sheep to pastures high in the Sierra Nevada, and presumably Sirretta Peak, some forty miles to the northeast and midway between the North and South Forks of the Kern River, was named for Sarret. A former miner, Virgile Bernard, a native of Orcières in the Upper Alps, and his wife Blanche (Sarret) also settled in Poso Flat.

In the early 1880s Léopold Vignave, a native of Bayonne, in southwest France, became the proprietor of Granite Station, a stopping place in the rolling hills midway between Bakersfield and Linn's Valley. His hotel, restaurant, and barroom were especially lively in the springtime when sheep shearing and wool buying were underway at his corrals. Yet offsetting Vignave's success as a proprietor was the tragic death of his pregnant wife following a frightening encounter with a rattlesnake.

Eugène Verdier, a native of Gers in the Upper Pyrenees, and his wife Marie (Laborde) came to Granite Station in 1908. Upon arriving in Kern County in the 1880s he had engaged in sheep raising, but then he became a hotel owner in East Bakersfield. In addition to managing the hotel, restaurant, and store at the midway stopping point on the Bakersfield-Linn's Valley road, Verdier raised stock on a ranch within a few miles of Granite Station.

Vincent Mon, a native of Aramits, and his wife Catherine, a native of Arette, both in the Lower Pyrenees, settled on a Poso Creek ranch about eight miles southwest of Granite Station in the mid-1890s. Enduring geographical names—Mon Creek, Mon Canyon, and Mon Bluff—are reminiscent of this family of eleven children on Poso Creek. Mon had worked as a hired hand in order to accumulate the capital he needed to become a sheepman, but he suffered heavy losses during the hard times of the early 1890s. After he recovered from this setback he turned to ranching in the middle of the decade.

Likewise the Tehachapi Mountains, at the southern end of the San Joaquin Valley, attracted a number of French stockmen, the earliest to arrive coming in the 1850s. François Channac, a native of Lespic in the Ardèche region, probably first saw these mountains in the mid-1850s. With George Cummings he crossed the range while driving cattle from southern to northern California. With Channac when he settled in Cummings Valley was a Spanish widow, Ramona Bello, and her daughter Refugia.

French Stockmen In Kern

If he tarried too long in a saloon, reportedly Ramona came, "slapped him about a bit," and hauled him away in a buckboard. Interestingly enough, by the mid-1870s Channac was the second wealthiest Frenchman in Kern County.

Among Channac's neighbors in Cummings Valley was Martin Mouliot, a native of Oloron Ste. Marie in the Lower Pyrenees. After reaching the valley in the early 1870s he worked as a hired hand until he could buy his own ranch. Later he married Refugia Bello. Another of the Cummings Valley settlers was Pierre Bernamayou, also a native of Oloron Ste. Marie, whose work as a hired hand enabled him to acquire his own ranch.

Although Germain Pellissier had been a Kern County sheepman in the 1870s, he became better known as the proprietor of the Pellissier Dairy in Los Angeles County. Yet several of his relatives settled in the Tehachapi Mountains. Among them was François Pellissier, a native of the Upper Alps, who settled in Cummings Valley, where his name in corrupted form was given to Pellisier Road. Late in the 1930s his ranch was acquired by a nephew, Jean Prel, also a native of the Upper Alps, who for several years had worked for the Pellissier Dairy. Prel and his wife Noémie (Moncoronel) were assisted by their son Jeannot in the management of the ranch. Another native of the Upper Alps, Nicolas Pellissier, late in the 1890s began to work for the dairy in Los Angeles, where he married Jeanne Seinturier. In the mid-1940s he bought ranch property in Brite's Valley, including the house of pioneer John M. Brite, which became the home of his son Jean and daughter-in-law Jeanne (Lagier).

In the 1870s brothers Bernard and Pierre Sartiat, who were natives of the Lower Pyrenees, settled on a Tehachapi Mountains ranch midway between Grapevine and San Emidio Canyons. Their livestock grazed along the courses of Tecuya and Salt Creeks. Farther west was the ranch of Alexis Godey, a well known "mountain man" who came to the area in the early 1850s. Born in Missouri of French Canadian parents, he turned from fur trading to ranching, first in Cuyama Valley, in the Coast Range. Later he moved to a ranch near San Emidio Canyon, in the Tehachapi Mountains. Another Frenchman attracted to the San Emidio area was Simon Bareille, who opened a store there in 1874 after having been in business at Panama with Lesser Hirschfeld, a native of Prussia. Yet in 1876 when Bareille registered to vote, he listed himself as a sheep raiser living at Sumner.

Although many of the French stockmen lived in the mountains that surrounded the San Joaquin Valley, some of them settled in the valley itself. Alexander Bergès, a native of Oloron Ste. Marie in the Lower Pyrenees, and his wife Margaret (Roquette) lived on a ranch about six miles south of Bakersfield. Bergès' father-in-law, Peter Prosper Roquette, and his wife Dora (Cervantes) for a time were the proprietors of Adobe Station, which was on the road that connected Bakersfield and Fort Tejon. They also operated sheep shearing corrals.

Peter Lambert, a native of Ancelle in the Upper Alps, began his career as a sheepman in the vicinity of Delano in the early 1870s, only to have ahead of him the problems of prolonged drought. He was in and out of the sheep business until 1908, but in the meantime he had acquired several thousand acres of land, some of which proved to be oil producing. He was living in East Bakersfield when he married Malvina Rambaud, a native of the Upper Alps.

Some of Kern County's French, from the time of their arrival, combined farming and sheep raising, while others engaged only in farming from the beginning. André André, a native of Gap in the Upper Alps, came to Kern County in the early 1870s, where he was joined by his brother Cyrille in the mid-1880s. After working for several years as sheepmen, the André brothers bought farms south of Bakersfield early in the twentieth century. At forty-eight years of age Cyrille married Marie Barthélemy, a native of the Upper Alps, who was twenty-five years his junior, and they became the parents of six children before his death in 1933. Some of their descendants are the proprietors of the André's Drive-Ins, and they are the producers of Frenchburgers.

Among the French farmers who settled in the Greenfield area was "Long Valley" Joe Eyraud, whose family name was so common that he adopted a sobriquet, one taken from the area in which he ran sheep. An uncle, Jean Pierre Lagier, was a miner at Rich Bar, on the Feather River in Plumas County, when Joseph's older brothers Iréné and François joined him. Finally, in the late 1880s, young Joseph gained family permission to emigrate, only to find that mining no longer was profitable, and he turned instead to sheep raising in Kern County. In 1910 he purchased a ranch at Greenfield, and in the following year he married Augustine Bertrand, a native of Chorges. They lived in a house built for an English lord who occupied it only briefly, and later it became the home of Eyraud's youngest daughter, Marguerite, and her husband, Michael Lorenzi. "Long Valley" Joseph Eyraud was a well known "witcher" who used a forked willow branch as a wand in his search for water, oil, gold, and silver. He died in 1948.

Another Joseph Eyraud came to Kern County in 1916 with his wife Emily (Prayer) and settled at Buttonwillow, where he was a pioneer cotton planter. Unfortunately for Eyraud wild rabbits ate the plants before the cotton could mature. He then moved to Weedpatch and raised sugar beets. Eyraud died in 1932, and his wife Emily subsequently married Peter Raymond.

Simon Richaud, a native of Romette in the Upper Alps, came to Kern County early in the twentieth century, and in 1914 he married Lucienne Le Flohic, whose family had come originally from the province of Brittany on the west coast of France. After herding sheep for a number of years, Richaud turned to farming on the southern outskirts of Bakersfield. A simple dirt farmer, he wore a tatooed ring in lieu of a wedding band and baked bread in an outdoor makeshift brick oven in the manner of the Upper Alps. Nine children were born to the Richauds at their farm on Planz Road, and in 1954 the homesite became the campus of South High School. Richaud's original acreage had been purchased from his brother-in-law, Joseph Escallier, whose wife Cécile was a twin sister of Lucienne. The Escalliers came to Kern County from Blackfoot, Idaho. Joseph was killed in an automobile accident in 1925, while returning from a Druids' picnic, and Simon died in 1962. The surviving widows, Lucienne and

Cécile, when in their nineties were indisputably the oldest twins in Kern County.

Lucien Le Flohic, the brother of twins Lucienne and Cécile, was a farmer living on Union Avenue near Bakersfield when he married his housekeeper, Mabel Hollis, who was a native of New Zealand. The youngest of their four children, Marie, became a talented acrobatic dancer. Her favorite feat was the spelling of her stage name, Marie Hollis, using her body to form the individual letters. While she was touring Europe in 1939, Adolph Hitler took a fancy to her, and he was entertained at a command performance. Known as America's dancing sweetheart, at the height of her fame she dabbled in motion pictures and was featured in *Life Magazine*. Marie Le Flohic had long been out of the public eye when she died in San Francisco in 1974.

After spending a quarter of a century in the sheep industry, Pierre Villard settled on a farm on Brundage Lane, near Union Avenue. He married Rose Grimaud and they became the parents of Peter and Rose. In 1914 Villard sold some acreage for the use of the Brundage School, and after the school had been relocated, his son Peter reacquired the property in 1940. In 1906 Maurice Nicolas ended a sheep-raising partnership with his brother-in-law André André and went for a short visit to France. When he returned he bought a ranch on Union Avenue. Another of the Union Avenue property owners was Désiré Ollivier, together with his wife Victorine (Nicolas), cousin of Louis Bécas, who was well known as a building contractor for the French community in Kern County.

Jacques and Jean Baptiste Oddous, who were brothers, came to Kern County in about 1900, arriving by way of Los Angeles. Upon giving up sheep raising for farming, they settled on farms in the Fruitvale area. Another pair of brothers was drawn to the Norris district, the first being Joseph Davin, who arrived in 1916. In the following year he was visited by his brother Pierre, who in 1919 returned and acquired a farm which adjoined that of his brother.

French Stockmen In Kern

Hippolyte Sarret, pioneer French sheepman, for whom Sirretta Peak in the Sierra Nevada was named. (Photo courtesy of Marie Bernard Schallock)

The French Ranch, located in the Greenhorn Mountains, homesteaded by Charles Caillaud in 1869. (Photo courtesy of Marie Bernard Schallock)

Frances (Guillon) Caillaud with her son Eugène at the French Ranch, circa 1885. (Photo courtesy of Marie Bernard Schallock)

Juliette "Julia" (Caillaud) Sarret with the Virgile Bernard family at Poso Flat in 1915. Left to right: Agnes Bernard, Juliette (Caillaud) Sarret, Blanche (Sarret) Bernard, Virgile Bernard holding daughter Marie. In front of Virgile: Joe Bernard, Blanche Bernard, and Albert Bernard. (Photo courtesy of Marie Bernard Schallock)

The Virgile Bernard home in the Greenhorn Mountains in 1918. Standing on the porch are daughters Blanche and Marie with their mother Blanche (Sarret) Bernard. (Photo courtesy of Marie Bernard Schallock)

The Martin Martin family in 1912. Back row: Augusta, Auguste, Helen. Front row: Alice, Anastasie (Escallier) Martin, Martin Jr. (Dolly), Martin Sr., Marie. (Photo courtesy of Auguste Martin)

Catherine Cazaux and Vincent Mon were married in 1887. (Photo courtesy of the Mon family)

Marie Laborde and Eugène Verdier were married in San Francisco on October 22, 1887. (Photo courtesy of Leah Provensal Castro)

François Channac, one of Kern County's richest Frenchmen until death and the railroad took everything he had. (Photo courtesy of Minnie Guhl Cesmat)

Ramona Bello rode over the Tehachapi Mountains with François Channac on the back of a mule. (Photo courtesy of Minnie Guhl Cesmat)

The Mouliots at home in Cummings Valley. Left to right: Laura, Frances, Refugia holding Charles, Amelia, Ida, Martin Jr., May, Martin Sr., and two hired hands. (Photo courtesy of Charlotte Lusk)

The children of Cyrille André at the time of Alice's First Communion. Back row: Frances and Mary. Front row: Alice, Cyril and Joe. (Photo courtesy of Leah Provensal Castro)

Dipping sheep. Far left: Octave Chastan. Far right: "Long Valley" Joe Eyraud. (Photo courtesy of Marguerite Eyraud Lorenzi)

François Eyraud mined for gold at Rich Bar on the Feather River in Plumas County while his younger brother "Long Valley" Joe turned to sheep raising. (Photo courtesy of Marguerite Eyraud Lorenzi)

A honeymoon photo of "Long Valley" Joe Eyraud, behind steering wheel, and his bride Augustine Bertrand. (Photo courtesy of Marguerite Eyraud Lorenzi)

Formerly owned by an English lord, the Greenfield home of "Long Valley" Joe Eyraud. Standing in photo: Augustine (Bertrand) Eyraud with Frank and Emily. (Photo courtesy of Marguerite Eyraud Lorenzi)

Joseph Eyraud, reportedly the first to grow sugar beets in Kern County, with his eight-mule team. (Photo courtesy of the Eyraud family)

The Joseph Eyraud home in Weedpatch, circa 1916. Left to right: Emily, Joe and Hank. (Photo courtesy of the Eyraud family)

Lest We Forget

The Prayer sisters, the future Marie Gil and the future Emily Eyraud. (Photo courtesy of Bertha Gil Crowley)

French Stockmen In Kern

Simon Richaud on his Planz Road acreage, circa 1934, later the site of South High School. (Photo courtesy of Louise Richaud)

The brick outdoor oven for baking bread located on the property of Simon Richaud. (Photo courtesy of Louise Richaud)

Kern County's oldest living twins as of 1978, Cécile and Lucienne Le Flohic, as they were in 1902. (Photo courtesy of Louise Richaud)

The Le Flohic twins, Cécile Escallier and Lucienne Richaud, circa 1952. (Photo courtesy of Louise Richaud)

Marie (Le Flohic) Hollis did a command performance for Hitler. Her acrobatic speciality was spelling her name using her body to form the letters. (Photo courtesy of Louise Richaud)

A Sartiat-Richaud family portrait. Left to right: Marie (Richaud) Boisseranc, Pierre Sartiat and his wife Marie Louise (Richaud) Sartiat, Bernard Sartiat, Bernard Pierre Sartiat, son of Pierre, who died in the epidemic of Spanish influenza after World War I at the age of twenty-five. (Photo courtesy of Dorita Boisseranc Iacopetti)

Lest We Forget

Jacques Oddous, circa 1918, with his first alfalfa crop. (Photo courtesy of Blanche Oddous Hughes)

CHAPTER IV

Along The Sheep Trails

Annually after the springtime lambing and shearing were over in the San Joaquin Valley, the flocks were grazed along at least a part of a four-hundred-mile-long trail that led to remote Inyo County, on the east side of the Sierra Nevada. One owner whose sheep spent "summer vacations" near Mono Lake, compared them to salmon which go out to feeding grounds in the ocean but eventually return to the place of their birth.

Sheep raising in Kern County had barely entered its third decade in the mid-1870s when a state-wide drought threatened to ruin the industry. In the hope of saving their starving flocks, French sheepmen, among others, drove their flocks to the already hard hit southern San Joaquin Valley. In an acrimonious article in mid-1877 the Bakersfield *Courier-Californian* reported that 10,000 unwelcome sheep had arrived whose herders "just moved fast enough...to clear off a large tract of country."

By the early 1870s feelings were running especially high against the interloping Frenchmen whose flocks, like the "locusts of Egypt," it was reported, devoured "everything before them." By hiding their flocks from the assessor, presumably they were avoiding the payment of taxes on them. Moreover, these "bedouins of the plains," it was charged, were enlarging their flocks by picking up stragglers and by allowing the mixing of flocks and then appropriating other herders' sheep while separating them.

The desperation of a Tehachapi Valley Frenchman over the plight of his drought-stricken sheep was reported by the Bakersfield *Kern County Gazette* in the fall of 1877. Augustin Bidabas and a partner cut down some 5,000 oak trees so that the starving sheep could eat the leaves. He was arrested by a deputy federal marshal, who charged him with unauthorized cutting of timber on the public domain.

Although the drought of the late 1870s ended, more difficulty was experienced by the Kern County sheepmen during the severe winter of 1881–1882, when a shortage of forage sent them out scouring the countryside for pasture for their starving sheep. When the sheep buyers arrived in the spring, many of the sheepmen were forced to sell at great loss. Some of the Frenchmen among them, with their fondest dreams shattered, returned to their homeland. For a few the outcome was unbearable, and they had to be committed to asylums.

Yet Mother Nature again favored the hard pressed sheepmen when a timely rain ended the drought early in 1884. How a group of elated Frenchmen celebrated the end of the anxious weather watch was recounted by the Bakersfield *Kern County Californian*. They came to town "in a slightly inebriated condition" and engaged in "loud and boisterous" singing, for which they were arrested and taken to jail. Then it became known that they were "respectable and well-to-do sheepmen" who were celebrating the coming of the "late rains," and they were freed "to sing until tired."

Although no one will ever know how many French herders were buried in unmarked graves along the desolate sheep trails, a few tragic deaths were recorded in the newspapers. For example late in 1890 the coroner investigated the suicide of Dominic Faure near Poso Creek, a herder who only recently had arrived from France. In commenting on his death the *Kern County Californian* called attention to the "absolutely contrasted" way of life in France and that in a sheep camp in California. For some, like the unfortunate herder who hanged himself in a cabin, the change could readily lead to "suicidal ideas." Another Frenchman, Frank Espitallier, died at William Scodie's ranch, in the South Fork Valley, late in 1891, from what the *Kern County Californian* presumed was pneumonia. He was found in his camp in "a dying condition" after his unattended sheep had wandered into an alfalfa field and several died of bloat.

Along The Sheep Trails

The financial problems of a seemingly wealthy Cummings Valley rancher only became fully apparent after the Frenchman died intestate late in 1892, leaving an estate valued between $11,000 and $15,000. François Channac's listed creditors resembled a Tehachapi "Who's Who," and the efforts to dispose of his estate dragged on for a decade. The chattel was sold in order to satisfy his indebtedness. Since a neighbor, Pierre Bernamayou, could not pay off a promissory note, his property was offered for sale. Then the Southern Pacific Railroad, holding that neither Channac nor Bernamayou had held valid titles to their land, appropriated both of the properties. Ultimately a residual few hundred dollars from Channac's estate were deposited in the county treasury. In 1902 some long lost heirs, two sisters and the children of a deceased brother, laid claim to the estate. A tempestuous legal battle established their claims, but after the legal fees were paid only a paltry inheritance was available to the heirs.

After they had enjoyed several years of prosperity in the late 1880s and early 1890s, Kern County's French sheepmen, among others, suffered a triple blow of adversity. By the provisions of the Wilson-Gorman Tariff, adopted in the summer of 1894, wool was placed on the duty-free list, thereby making it easier for foreign wool to compete for the American market. This congressional action was strongly opposed by the National Wool Growers' Association. The tariff measure went into force during the worst depression since the 1870s, with a resulting drop in the price and the market for wool. Further complicating the plight of the sheepmen was another drought, and they could not find sufficient grazing areas for their flocks in the spring of 1894. In a desperate attempt to save the industry, a group of financiers rented eighty double-deck freight cars to ship flocks to Colorado. By summer most of the sheepmen, large and small, were going out of business, some of them while trying to rescue their less fortunate compatriots.

The great mercantile firm of Beneditto Ardizzi and Louis Virgin Olcese, of East Bakersfield, which had bankrolled many of the sheepmen, declared bankruptcy in the summer of 1894.

Lest We Forget

During its reorganization there were foreclosures on some substantial promissory notes. Sheepmen long remembered this era of the so-called "Cleveland Bust."

Romulus Petrus Borel was a French sheepman whose economic reverses in the 1890s may well have determined the course of water development in southern California. He came from the Upper Alps as a youth to join his older brother Vincent in the Bishop area as a herder and eventually acquired considerable range land and water rights in the Owens Valley. Although he might have weathered the drought of the 1890s, he could not withstand the collapse of a Bishop bank. With other Owens Valley sheepmen, he lost his land and water rights. Afterwards William Mulholland began a quiet, but successful, campaign to acquire land and water rights in the valley on behalf of the burgeoning city of Los Angeles. In 1895 Borel and his wife Félicie (Espitallier) moved to the San Joaquin Valley where he began to farm near Bakersfield. Subsequently he worked for the Southern Pacific Railroad and the Ardizzi-Olcese mercantile firm.

Once the hard times of the mid-1890s were over, the most indomitable of the French sheepmen rebuilt their flocks in the late 1890s. Others turned to farming, never again having anything to do with the sheep industry, or turned to business careers. A few became "colorful figures" and whiled away their time as patrons of the French-owned saloons or played boules or bocces* on vacant lots. Among those who could not face unhappy reality was one for whom, as the *Kern County Californian* reported in mid-1894, "the air was peopled with materialized spirits with whom he had endless converse." Yet during the prosperous years ahead, which lasted until the outbreak of World War I, a new wave of Frenchmen reached Kern County, the bulk of them coming from the Upper Alps and Lower Pyrenees.

---

* The Alpine French preferred the Italian name of the bowling game and also used the larger Italian balls made from the hand-rubbed burls of trees. "Bocces," it should be noted, is a dialectal variant used by the Alpine French and their descendants.

Three French sheepherders in a lighter moment. Left to right: Fidèle Rostain, Jean Espitallier, Joe Vieux. The boy is unknown. (Photo courtesy of the Aubin family)

Three French sheepherders with dog and pack mules at Piute Creek, in 1908. Left to right: Frank Espitallier, Fidèle Provensal, and Etienne Espitallier. (Photo courtesy of Etienne Espitallier)

Joseph Espitallier once lost an entire flock of sheep in a hail storm. (Photo courtesy of Dolly Espitallier Ansolabehere)

The wedding picture of Romulus Petrus Borel and Félicie Rosalie Espitallier, taken in 1891. Their attendants are unidentified. (Photo courtesy of Ernest and Marcelle Reynaud Borel.)

A sheep camp in the Bishop area in 1916. Left to right: Louis Roux, Louis Borel, Etienne Espitallier, André Escallier, Auguste Philipp, Jeannette Philipp, Jean "Sprit" Espitallier, Marie Roux. (Photo courtesy of Etienne Espitallier)

Baking shepherd's bread in the McFarland area in 1937. Left to right: Jean Raymond Jr., Rose Raymond, Frank Saulque, Pete Raymond, Ernest Bresson Jr., Ernest Bresson Sr., Marie Raymond, Armand Reynier, Suzie Bresson, Jean Utural, Joe Bresson. Squatting: Jean Raymond Sr. and Marius Roux. (Photo courtesy of Blanche Reynaud Borda)

Ready for the Bastille Day parade, circa 1914. Standing at attention in the bocce court next to the French House on East 21st Street are, left to right: Henri Espitallier, Jules Delagne, Joe Vivian Sr., Frank Alexis, "Gros" Jean Espitallier, Joe Vivian Jr., Louis Bécas, Elysée Galland, Ambroise Vivian, Joe Espitallier, Fidèle Rostain, Joe Bresson, Louis Chauvet. (Photo courtesy of Val Vivian)

CHAPTER V

Havilah: A Mining Town

When the Civil War began in the early 1860s, it became obvious that a high percentage of the miners on the Kern River were in support of the South. For this reason the anti-secessionists were alarmed over the migration of miners to Clear Creek, in the mountains south of Keyesville, late in 1864. Supposedly the secessionists were rallying there on behalf of the South under the leadership of Asbury Harpending, a notorious conspirator who had tried to sail a Confederate privateer from San Francisco Bay. Then late in 1865 it became known that prospectors had found promising gold deposits on Clear Creek. In anticipation of a gold excitement, Harpending laid out a town, which he gave the biblical name of Havilah. The Civil War was over when, with a fortune of $800,000 amassed from the sale of town lots, he returned to San Francisco. The Clear Creek mining boom helped bring about the creation of Kern County in mid-1866, with its county seat placed at Havilah.

Not only were Frenchmen like Dr. Claude de la Borde and Auguste Gouglat among the discoverers of the mines along Clear Creek, but some of Havilah's leading businessmen also were Frenchmen. One of these was Léopold Wattier, the proprietor of the Golden Gate Hotel on Main Street. He was assisted in the hosting by his wife Augustine. In the Havilah *Courier* Wattier advertised that he provided "good rooms and clean beds." Meals were "served at all hours—cooking done in French style."

In the summer of 1869 Wattier erected a two-story building on a lot adjoining the Golden Gate Hotel. The lower floor was used for dancing and the upper one was used as a meeting hall by the Independent Order of Odd Fellows. Among the town's outstanding social events was a grand ball given at the Golden Gate Hotel in the spring of 1873 in celebration of the founding of Odd Fellowship in the United States. The Havilah *Miner* reported that Wattier had provided everything that was necessary for "the pleasure of his guests." During a temporary suspension of the dancing soon after midnight a delicious dinner was served, and then the dancing continued until "the shades of night had nearly flown."

Another of Havilah's French businessmen was Jacob Asher, who with a succession of partners, beginning with William G. Sanderson, was the co-proprietor of the Billiard Saloon on Main Street. According to an advertisement in the Havilah *Courier*, patrons could "while away an hour very pleasantly" at their billiard tables, and the choicest brands of whiskey and wine were available at the bar. After a special social event at the Billiard Saloon in the summer of 1868, the *Courier* reported that the jovial Asher had served a "fine lunch," and drinks "of superior quality flowed freely." Helping to improve the quality of life at Havilah were French tradesmen like François Escaiche, who, when not engaged in mining, worked as a baker, and Jacob Rantz, who found employment as a cook.

The mining boom that had brought about Havilah's founding and the creation of Kern County in the mid-1860s was on the decline by the end of that decade. In the meantime Bakersfield, an agricultural trading center, had been founded on the lower reaches of the Kern River, and around it was promising agricultural land in the southern San Joaquin Valley. By the fall of 1869 some of Havilah's businessmen had moved to Bakersfield, including the proprietor of the Havilah *Courier*, who renamed it the *Kern County Courier*. In addition to Havilah's economic decline there was a weakening political position as well, which led to a bitter contest over the removal of the county seat to Bakersfield. The move was made early in 1874.

The Havilah *Miner*, a newspaper which in its founding was expected to champion the interests of the declining town, reported in mid-1874 that Jacob Asher's Billiard Saloon had

Havilah: A Mining Town

"expired." The *Miner* itself had ceased publication when the *Courier*, in the fall of 1875, reported that Léopold Wattier had sold the Golden Gate Hotel and moved to San Francisco. Although the best mines of the southern Sierra Nevada continued to produce satisfactorily for several more years, there was a growing emphasis upon agricultural developments in Kern County starting in the early 1870s.

CHAPTER VI

Bakersfield: The Emerging San Joaquin

In the fall of 1863 Col. Thomas Baker moved from Visalia to the lower reaches of the Kern River, where he began to reclaim the swamp and overflow land of the so-called Kern Island in the southern San Joaquin Valley. "The latch string of his abode," it was commonly known, "was always out." The colonel and his wife Ellen generously entertained travelers at their home and invited them to pasture their teams in Baker's field. Understandably, when a Kern Island town was laid out in the mid-1860s, it was named Bakersfield. The town's pioneer businessmen, Horatio P. Livermore and Julius Chester, in the late 1860s were joined by some merchants who came from Havilah.

Among the businessmen who were attracted to Bakersfield was Ernest Escalet, a former miner who sought to fare better through his skill with a crepe pan than a gold pan. He became the celebrated proprietor of the French Restaurant. In the spring of 1873 Escalet expanded his business role to include that of hotelman, and, as was recounted in doggerel verse,

> ... they raised up quite a structure,
>   that stood for many a day,
> 'Twas builded by John Howlett, for that
>   Frenchman "Escalet."
> 'Twas a place of some importance, and many
>   knew it well,
> All through this southern country as "the
>   old French Hotel."

The French Hotel, located conveniently at the corner of 19th Street and Chester Avenue, was opened in the summer of 1873. Escalet not only thanked his friends for their "liberal support" of the French Restaurant, but he also expressed the hope that he would "merit the same liberal patronage at the French Hotel." Yet within two months he was seeking a buyer for the hotel because, as the *Kern County Courier* explained, it was necessary for him to go to Europe "on important business."

Although Escalet had been the proprietor of the French Hotel for only a short time, its fine reputation for elegant furnishings and cuisine were continued under non-French ownership. It was the scene of such French social festivities as the Réveillons or Christmas Eve parties. Moreover in the pre-railroad era the hotel was the headquarters for the stage companies that connected Bakersfield with Havilah, Kernville, Lone Pine, and Los Angeles.

When the county seat was moved to Bakersfield early in 1874, a celebration ball was held to commemorate the event. Although the dancing took place at the Town Hall, the dinner was served at the French Hotel. Ernest Escalet was in town again, and the *Courier* praised the resourcefulness and "artistic skills" of the Frenchman. The newspaper asserted that the ball was "the most successful" social event held so far in Bakersfield.

With some of his townsmen Escalet moved to booming Caliente, at the Southern Pacific's railhead near Tehachapi Pass, but after the boom was over he resumed his role as the illustrious chef of Bakersfield. In mid-1876 he leased the restaurant in the Arlington House, and, in quarters described by the *Courier-Californian* as "fitted up in elegant style," he promised to give "undivided... attention to the cooking department." Yet within two months he had moved across Chester Avenue and opened another restaurant, La Maison Dorée, next door to the French Hotel.

Well known among Kern County's French merchants was Alphonse Weill, a native of the small Alsatian town of Wolfisheim, located near the present-day German border. After a brief stay in San Francisco, which he reached in 1870, he went to Havilah and found employment with the help of an uncle, Jacob Asher. In 1872 Weill came to Bakersfield, where he was employed by Jacob Weil, a merchant who, in spite of the simi-

Bakersfield: The Emerging San Joaquin

larity of names, was not a relative. They became partners in mid-1874, and subsequently Weill acquired the business, located on 19th Street, between Chester Avenue and K Street.

Two years after Weill replaced his wooden building with a brick one, it was destroyed in a widespread fire in mid-1889 and he rebuilt the structure in an even grander style. In accordance with the credit practices of the time he bankrolled many of the sheepmen and farmers during the lean years, and this brought him close to bankruptcy in the hard times of the early 1890s. Yet he weathered that and other crises during his many years as a leading businessman in Kern County.

In 1882 Alphonse Weill married Henrietta Lévy, whose family he had met when he first arrived in San Francisco. They lived at the corner of 17th and H Streets, where they became the parents of four children. After Weill's death in 1946 his son Lawrence, who had been a business associate for several years, managed the firm until it was dissolved in 1952.

The Weill home site was purchased from Alexis Godey, a native of St. Louis whose parents were French Canadians. While engaged in fur trading he became familiar with western geography, and, starting in the early 1840s, he guided several of Captain John C. Frémont's expeditions into the West. In the early 1850s Godey came to the Tehachapi Mountains and worked as an Indian agent under Lieutenant Edward F. Beale. He had lived on a ranch near San Emidio Canyon for many years, when, in the mid-1880s, he moved to Bakersfield and lived on 19th Street, near Central Park. When the Mexican War veterans, including Generals Frémont and Beale, as well as Godey, were granted pensions in 1887, the two generals assigned their pensions to their friend Godey. While Godey was seeking medical help at Sisters' Hospital in Los Angeles, he died early in 1889.

Auguste P. Eyraud, a native of Gap in the Upper Alps, was another of Bakersfield's prominent French businessmen, especially as a hotelman and liquor dealer. He arrived in San Francisco in the early 1870s, and, after a few years of employment as a hotel and tannery worker, he opened the Hôtel des Alpes on

Pacific Street. Upon coming to Bakersfield in 1880 Eyraud became the proprietor of the Alps Hotel, on the corner of 19th and M Streets. His hotel was destroyed in the fire of 1889, and he built a new one across the street and named it the French Hotel. This one was also consumed by fire in 1900, and after it was rebuilt he named it the Commercial Hotel. In 1909, while it was leased, he built the St. Regis Hotel on adjoining property. In the meantime Eyraud, in the mid-1880s, had opened the French Liquor Store, as well as become an agent for a brewery firm. He advertised that he was the pioneer liquor dealer in Bakersfield. In 1912 he retired from the liquor business and concentrated on the management of his business, ranch, and oil properties which were in various parts of Kern County.

Early in 1884 Auguste P. Eyraud married Rosalie Caillaud, a native of Paris, France, who was the daughter of Charles Caillaud, owner of the French Ranch in the Greenhorn Mountains. After first living in a house at the corner of 17th and M Streets, not far from Eyraud's hotel, the family moved to a larger house at the corner of Truxtun Avenue and N Street. The Eyrauds' son died as a teenager, and their daughter Alice Ingram only outlived her father by eleven years, the same number of years that she was survived by her mother.

Jean Baptiste Bergès, a native of Oloron Ste. Marie in the Lower Pyrenees, was another of Bakersfield's liquor dealers. Upon reaching Kern County in the late 1880s, he became associated with his older brother, Alexander Bergès, in ranching near Bakersfield. Late in 1889, after he had left ranching and was dealing in liquor, he rented quarters in Alphonse Weill's restored building on 19th Street. In the following year he married Marie Inda, a native of Aldudes, a small town from which many French Basques eventually came to Kern County. She was the eldest of four sisters, three of whom came to Bakersfield after the marriage of a relative, Marianne Laxague, to Pablo Galtes, a native of Barcelona, Spain, who was a pioneer merchant in Bakersfield.

The Bergès family was living in a house at the corner of 19th and D Streets when a Valentine's Day, 1893, reception was held

Bakersfield: The Emerging San Joaquin

following the marriage of Marie's sister Louise to Faustino Noriega. That same year Noriega left the employ of Miller and Lux, a great landholding firm, to build and become the proprietor of the Iberia Hotel in East Bakersfield.

Many segments of the town's closely-knit ethnic community—French, Basque, and Spanish—attended this social event. In 1894 Bergès moved his family into a larger house on the opposite side of the street in order to have more room for his six children. After Marie's death he married Grace Bergerette, but he died soon afterwards in 1916.

Octave Roux, a native of Théus in the Upper Alps, was a teenager when he reached San Francisco in 1885, and then his search for work took him to Oregon and Washington. While he was cutting timber in northern California and carrying a gun for his personal safety, he decided that was not the sort of life he wanted. In 1893 he took the advice of some fellow Frenchmen and went to Bakersfield, where he was employed as a bartender by Auguste P. Eyraud, for whom he had worked briefly in San Francisco. Subsequently in a building owned by his friend and benefactor Eyraud, Roux entered the grocery business on 19th Street, between M and N Streets.

In the fall of 1895, Octave Roux married Louise Philipp,* who was a sister of Jean Philipp, one of the leading sheepmen of Kern County. After living temporarily in quarters at the rear of the store, they moved to a house on Truxtun Avenue, between M and N Streets, where six children were born, four of whom survived to adulthood. After Roux died in 1921, his sons Louis and Ernest remained in the grocery business until 1924. In the 1920s Louis became a dealer in sporting goods, and in the 1930s Ernest went into the furniture business. After the death of Auguste P. Eyraud's daughter Alice Ingram in 1933, the former Roux Grocery Store was taken over by Joseph and Peter Belluomini, who operated it as the City Grocery. This was one of the many instances in which a French family was supplanted by an

---

* The missing "e" at the end of the family name was restored by the descendants.

Italian family in the changing ownership of business in Kern County.

Not all of Bakersfield's French businessmen were hotelmen, merchants, liquor dealers, and restaurant owners, as a check of the newspaper advertisements and business directories reveals. When Bakersfield was a fledgling village in the early 1870s, Léon Cordier operated a tonsorial parlor in the rear part of John G. and George W. Tungate's saloon, on Chester Avenue. Antoine P. Toussaint, until he returned to France in the mid-1880s, worked as a tinsmith at his shop on 19th Street. On that same street, in the 1890s, was Auguste Amar's Parisian Bakery. Armand Ducommun, a watchmaker and jeweler, in business by the 1890s on Chester Avenue, continued in his trade until the 1920s. Early in the 1920s Auguste Ariey, Auguste M. Michel, both Alpine French, and John B. Martinto, a French Basque, became the proprietors of the Bakersfield Seed and Feed Store on 19th Street. Especially with the beginning of the Kern River oil boom in 1900 Bakersfield had an extensive and bawdy tenderloin district. In the heyday of this "sporting town" at least two French-descended madams, Marie-Thérèse Brignaudy and Madame de Yough, managed brothels. Visits to the madams cost three dollars, while visits to the so-called "cribs" cost one dollar. However, it was well known that most of the "crib" girls made more money by "rolling the drunks."

Octave Roux in his grocery store at 1123 19th Street. (Photo courtesy of Marie Roux Hardwick)

The Roux family at home on Truxtun Avenue in 1907. Left to right: Louis, Louise holding Irene, Octave, Berthe Espitallier (cousin of Louise (Philipp) Roux), and Ernest. Seated on carpet: Marie. (Photo courtesy of Marie Roux Hardwick)

The French Hotel of Bakersfield, built in 1873, on the corner of 19th Street and Chester Avenue. (Photo courtesy of the Kern County Museum)

The Weill Brothers' General Merchandise Store. (Photo courtesy of Lawrence Weill)

The Weill Block on 19th Street between Chester Avenue and G Street. (Photo courtesy of Lawrence Weill)

Inside the Weill Store. (Photo courtesy of Lawrence Weill)

The wedding picture of Louise Philipp and Octave Roux taken in 1895. (Photo courtesy of Marie Roux Hardwick)

The "new" French Hotel at 19th and M Streets. Auguste Pierre Eyraud, proprietor, in buckboard. (Photo courtesy of Jeanne Abadie Edmondson)

Inside A. P. Eyraud's saloon at 19th and M Streets in 1900, before electricity had been installed. Tending bar: Joseph Faure. First man at bar: A. P. Eyraud. (Photo courtesy of Jeanne Abadie Edmondson)

Inside A. P. Eyraud's saloon in April 1909. A. P. Eyraud tending bar. Note electric lights. (Photo courtesy of Jeanne Abadie Edmondson)

The first residence of the A. P. Eyraud family at 17th and M Streets. Left to right: Alice, August, Rosalie (Caillaud) Eyraud and Auguste Pierre Eyraud. (Photo courtesy of Marie Bernard Schallock)

Bakersfield: The Emerging San Joaquin

The Bergès family. Standing: Jean Baptiste and Baptiste "Bap." Seated: Alexander, Mother Bergès, and Jean Pierre.

The Noriega wedding reception held at the Jean Baptiste Bergès residence on the corner of 19th and D Streets. Background on left: Mother Bergès, Jean Baptiste Bergès holding son George, Marie (Inda) Bergès. Wedding party: Justo Mouesca, Faustino Noriega, Louise (Inda) Noriega, Marie (Inda) Jauregui. Priest: Father Gannon. On porch: Pablo Galtes (in foreground); in back of him, Auguste Pierre Eyraud and Rosalie (Caillaud) Eyraud. (Photo courtesy of Marie Bernard Schallock)

Jean Baptiste Bergès and Marie Inda were married November 20, 1890. (Photo courtesy of Minnie Guhl Cesmat)

CHAPTER VII

French Settlers Of North Kern

While southbound construction on the Southern Pacific Railroad was underway in the early 1870s, several new towns were founded by the company in the San Joaquin Valley. One of these was Delano, a few miles within the bounds of Kern County, where construction was halted for about a year during the Panic of 1873. While this settlement was the railhead it was a "very lively spot," according to the Bakersfield *Kern County Courier*, and it was "constantly thronged with teams delivering and receiving freight." The town was named for Columbus Delano, who was the Secretary of the Interior under President Ulysses S. Grant. The family name had French roots, being originally De la Noye, but it was changed after his Huguenot ancestors sought to avoid religious persecution by coming to the United States.

From the time of its founding in the early 1870s some of the leading businessmen of Delano were Frenchmen. Foremost among these was Emile Chauvin, a native of southern France, who was a child when his father, Jovin Chauvin, an outspoken journalist, exiled himself to Cuba in the late 1840s. While yet a teenager the younger Chauvin went to gold-rush California. In 1854, after spending some time at San Jose, Monterey, Sacramento, and San Juan Capistrano, he went to La Grange, on the Tuolumne River, a settlement at first called French Bar. There he engaged in mining, cattle raising, and store keeping. At La Grange he married a Parisian who bore him a son, Emile André, before she died in 1861.

In 1873 Chauvin moved to newly-founded Delano, then a busy railhead, where he was in business until 1900. His general store, hotel, and livery stable were located on Front Street near the Southern Pacific depot. In the midst of overall business success, however, Chauvin suffered serious personal and material losses. His son, Emile André, who had attended Santa Clara College, became mentally deranged and died in Santa Clara County in mid-1885. In the summer of 1890 Delano underwent the scourge of fire, a fate that many frontier towns experienced. According to a report in the Bakersfield *Kern County Californian*, the holocaust started in Chauvin's barn and "spread with great rapidity . . . in an incredibly short time." Although most of the town was saved from destruction, only "a heap of cinders and ashes" remained along much of Front Street.

In 1900 Chauvin sold his business to an employee, Frank Claudino, a native of Portugal, and retired to Delonegha Hot Springs, a mountain resort in the Kern River Canyon. When he died intestate in 1902 an appraisal was made of his estate, including a sizeable piece of real estate. An investigation revealed that this property had been sold to the Delano Realty Company, which belatedly found that the title was faulty and took steps to quiet it.

Another of Delano's pioneer businessmen was an enigmatic Frenchman, Adrien Defos du Rau, the owner of the French Hotel. In the summer of 1876 he advertised in the Bakersfield *Kern County Gazette* that his hotel was "kept in the best style," and his restaurant served the "best the market afforded." Jean Adrien Mandis was associated with him in at least some of his enterprises, including sheep shearing corrals near Delano. In the spring of 1877 Mandis reported to the *Kern County Gazette* that approximately 100,000 sheep would be sheared at the town. In later years that figure rose to 225,000. In 1879 du Rau was in serious financial trouble, being charged with fraud by his creditors, who sued him. Although at an early trial he was found not guilty, he had continuing financial problems in the early 1880s. He died early in 1884 at the age of fifty-six in Delano.

In the meantime the star of his associate, Jean Adrien Mandis, was ascending at Delano. A native of Mézin, France, as a young man he had jumped ship on the California coast in order

French Settlers Of North Kern

to join a brother in the mines of Calaveras County. While engaged in mining he learned the butchering and baking trades. From 1868 to 1872 he lived at Hornitos in Mariposa County, and then he stayed briefly at Snelling in Merced County, where he kept the Planter's Hotel. Doubtless in both Hornitos and Snelling he met businessmen who later were prominent in Kern County, where he went late in 1874 to manage the Railroad Hotel at Sumner. This newly-founded railroad town a mile and a half east of Bakersfield later became East Bakersfield. After a brief stay at Sumner Mandis went to Delano, where he was employed by du Rau. In 1875 he married Frances Saiz, the daughter of a Peruvian, Pedro Saiz, who was then a hotelkeeper at Snelling.

Late in 1883 the *Kern County Californian* reported that Mandis had been declared an insolvent debtor and Emile Chauvin was the assignee of his estate. Yet early in the next year the same newspaper announced that Mandis had been discharged from insolvency just prior to the death of du Rau. In the summer of 1884 Chauvin, as assignee, sold enough real estate to satisfy Mandis' indebtedness.

In the meantime Mandis had been "doing business as usual" at Delano. In the spring of 1884 he advertised in the *Kern County Californian* that his hotel had been "thoroughly renovated and improved," and that he had excellent facilities for the "shearing and dipping of sheep." Available at his "good stable" was plenty of stock feed, as well as good horses and spring wagons for hire.

Besides his occasional involvements as plaintiff and defendant, Mandis sometimes served as a witness in court cases involving violence at Delano. In the summer of 1885 he was an acting justice of the peace. His court-related role is narrated in the Delano Historical Society's *The Plow* for September 1975. Moreover Mandis, together with young Emile André Chauvin, represented the Delano precinct at the Democratic political convention held at Bakersfield late in 1884. Unexpectedly Mandis died in the spring of 1888 at Porterville, where he had real estate interests. His beautiful pipe-smoking widow, Frances, and his surviving five children remained at Delano for two more years, where she managed the Brown House before moving to Los Angeles.

Delano was barely in its second decade of growth when a reporter for the Stockton *Interior*, in mid-1885, visited the town and the surrounding countryside. He observed that there were several business establishments at this trading center with importance for its sheep shearing and wool shipping facilities. Settlement was underway on nearby farms, and this development was affording increasing economic benefits for Delano. The journalist visited Emile Chauvin's thriving garden, vineyard, and orchard, which were a short distance from the town. When told that water was available at from twenty-five to thirty feet below the ground surface, he urged the use of windmills, as was the case in the "windmill city" of Stockton. After visiting Delano the journalist understood the wisdom of buying cheap land in Kern County rather than the more expensive land elsewhere in California.

Especially in the 1880s there was an influx of Frenchmen to the Delano area, and almost all of them came from the Champsaur Valley in the Upper Alps. One of these was Ambroise Villard, the oldest of nine children, who decided "to try his fortune" in California. At first he lived in Ventura County, where he worked for wages until he could acquire his own sheep. In the early 1880s Villard moved his headquarters to Delano and began to purchase land east of town, in the vicinity of Rag Gulch. Early in the twentieth century he turned to cattle raising—from herding to ranching—and his "VA" brand was well known in the Sierra Nevada foothills. Also he became a stockholder in the First National Bank of Delano, as well as a director of the telephone company that linked Delano and Linn's Valley. Meanwhile, in 1887, he had married Eugénie Marie Faure, a native of the Upper Alps, and with the birth of eleven children they comprised one of the largest French families in Kern County.

In the early 1880s four Faure brothers, natives of Saint Julien in the Upper Alps, began to graze sheep in the San Joaquin

French Settlers Of North Kern

Valley. Cyril settled in Porterville, while his brothers Pierre, François, and Joseph lived in Delano. Eventually Pierre and Joseph sold their flocks and opened a store on High Street, and they not only sold merchandise, but they also bankrolled many of the local sheepmen. In 1904 the brothers sold their business to André Vieux.

In the late 1880s André Vieux, a native of Saint Laurent in the Upper Alps, came to Delano and engaged in sheep herding. The capital he accumulated with the expectation of buying his own flock was lost during the depression of the early 1890s. Yet by the middle of that decade he had recovered financially and he began to buy ranch and commercial property. Vieux bought the Faure brothers' store in 1904 and the Delano Hardware store in 1906. Continuing the practice of his predecessors, he bankrolled sheepmen, and he was an organizer-director of the First National Bank of Delano. In 1909 he married Anaïs Rostain, the widow of Célestin Rostain and cousin of Ambroise Villard. During her widowhood she had operated a boardinghouse and laundry in order to support her five children. She was a native of the Upper Alps.

Another Frenchman who began life in America as a sheepman but turned to business was Auguste Perrier. A native of St. Bonnet in the Upper Alps, he arrived in Kern County in the mid-1870s. With his wife Angéline Oddous Sommers Poncelet, he was the proprietor of a saloon on 10th Street, a half a block from the Southern Pacific depot. Saloons were more numerous than churches, and there was a brief period, well in advance of national prohibition, when Delano went "dry." A local option measure went into force early in 1912, and the Delano *Record* announced the closing of the saloons. Without his "plans formulated," Perrier was bewildered, not knowing what he would do under the circumstances. With the repeal of the short-lived measure, however, Delano again became "wet," and it was business as usual until the adoption of national prohibition early in 1920. Auguste Perrier's father, Joseph, came to Delano after his wife's death in 1906, and he was followed by relatives, including Paulin and Auguste Dusserre, who located nearby.

Lest We Forget

Four of the Girard brothers, of a family of eight boys and one girl, left Ancelle in the Upper Alps for the United States, the first being the oldest, Emile, who went to San Francisco. The next oldest, Philippe, reached Delano in the mid-1880s, and during the next few years he was joined there by his younger brothers Joseph and Jules. These three brothers were partners in the sheep business until Jules branched out on his own in the early 1890s. Philippe and Joseph acquired a ranch some sixteen miles west of Delano, while Jules' ranch was about the same distance east of town. The brothers married women from their native province—Philippe to Anaïs Brochier, Joseph to Eve Chabot, and Jules to Thérèse Marie Motte. A sheepman's wife not only raised the children, but she also was a silent partner in the ranch activity. While the flocks were nearby during the lambing and shearing season, Anaïs, for example, cooked meals for the herders of as many as 12,000 sheep.

Unlike many of his compatriots at Delano, who were natives of the Upper Alps, Auguste Borel was a native of Coligny, a small town northeast of Lyon. Yet his mother was from the Upper Alps. When he first visited Delano in the early 1880s, he stayed only a short time, but he returned in the middle of that decade and herded sheep. In 1906, after a few years as manager of a small hotel in Angiola in Tulare County, Borel established the Delano Hotel at the corner of 10th and Main Streets. In the meantime he had married Marie Labarthe, a native of Lasseube in the Lower Pyrenees, who came to Delano from San Francisco after a doctor recommended a warmer climate. The Borel daughters, Louise (Panero) and Martha (Woollomes), long remembered standing on the hotel balcony in order to count the approaching wagons so that their mother could know how many diners to expect. After her husband's death Marie, with the help of her son-in-law Frank Panero, continued to run the hotel. She was 101 years of age when she died in 1971.

Among Delano's early-day hotels was the Escallier, named for brothers Léon, Jules, and Antoine Escallier, who probably arrived in the mid-1880s. Antoine and Jules eventually went to San Francisco and left Léon in charge of their properties in

French Settlers Of North Kern

Kern County. He married Louise Borel, the sister of hotelman Auguste Borel, and after Léon's death she married Pierre Faure. With his Swiss wife Ida (Moreau), Jules, by then the surviving brother, returned to Delano at the turn of the century and managed the hotel, and Pierre and Louise moved to Oakland. After the death of Jules in 1902, Ida married Albert Castagnet, a native of the Lower Pyrenees, who was a vaudeville performer.

Wherever there is at least a handful of French people, there is usually a French bakery as well. Marcel Reynaud, a native of St. Bonnet in the Upper Alps, followed his two older brothers Auguste and Jean to Delano, where they were sheepherders. However, he preferred to do other kinds of work, and became a clerk at the New Central Hotel in the employ of André Vieux. Early in 1909 the Delano *Record* announced that Reynaud was opening a "first class bakery" on the west side of Delano. Later he moved to East Bakersfield and was in and out of the baking business until he was employed at Union Cemetery, where he worked until his death in 1955.

Among Delano's skilled tradesmen was Joseph Bertrand, born in Orcières in the Upper Alps, who had learned the cobbler's trade while serving in the French army. He came to the United States intending only to visit his sister Marie DeVoto, who then was living at Delano, but his visit lasted a lifetime. At first he herded sheep, but later he plied his trade as a cobbler. Bertrand married Anaïs Aubin, who had followed her brother, Pierre Jean Aubin, to East Bakersfield, where she was employed in a hotel. In 1921, when the Bertrands, then the parents of seven children, needed a larger house, they bought one on Kensington Street from another Frenchman, Auguste "By Thunder" Lagier.

Best known by his sobriquet, Auguste "By Thunder" Lagier was a Delano sheepman who at the age of sixty-five made a flying leap at Famoso for a moving train that was bound for Delano. Because of his age and weight he slipped and fell under a wheel, and as a consequence he lost his right leg. "By Thunder" was well-known for his vocal proposals, sometimes made in fun and sometimes seriously. Doubtless in jest he proposed the renaming of the street on which he lived Lagier or "By Thunder" Street. On the other hand, he was one of the serious advocates of artesian wells as a source of water for flour milling at Delano.

In the meantime Famoso had been founded about eleven miles south of Delano, at a watering place commonly used by French sheepherders. Originally it was a Southern Pacific station called Poso, after nearby Poso Creek, but the name was easily confused with Pozo in San Luis Obispo County. Consequently it was elegantly renamed Spottiswood, but that designation soon lost out to the more popular Famoso. With the coming of settlers to the surrounding area early in the twentieth century, businesses fronting on the railroad were established.

As was the case in Delano, the Pacific Improvement Company, a Southern Pacific subsidiary, owned most of the property on either side of the Southern Pacific railway. It was not until 1910, when a wave of homesteaders flocked to the area, that the business portion of the town began to develop and rights to property fronting the railroad tracks were first sold.

Two French families especially retained a long association with Famoso—the Orciers and the Cesmats. In the early 1890s Romulus Orcier, a native of Bussard in the Upper Alps, joined his brothers Fred and Théophile, who were herding sheep on Poso Creek, In mid-1930 Romulus married Marie Mélanie Morel, a native of Los Angeles, who was the daughter of Julien Morel, a stockman who came to Kern County in the late 1880s. Following his marriage, Orcier sold his sheep and opened the Pioneer Hotel, together with a saloon and a livery stable, at Famoso. Since he was one of the last in the county to lose his liquor license, his saloon did a thriving business with the approach of prohibition in 1920. Subsequently he opened a store and service station. Three children were born to the Orciers—Clementine, Julia, and Romulus. The Orciers lived out their lives in Famoso, where Romulus died early in 1944 and his wife in mid-1959.

The other longtime French family which resided at Famoso was that of Joseph Cesmat, a native of Gap in the Upper Alps.

French Settlers Of North Kern

His wife Juliette was the daughter of Jules and Ida Escallier of Delano. He succeeded in becoming a sheep owner in the early 1890s, but he lost his investment during the depression that came early in that decade and spent the rest of his active life as a herder. His wife died in the influenza epidemic at the end of World War I, leaving him a widower with three small sons—Jules, Joe, and Louis. The Orciers helped raise his children while he continued to earn a living herding sheep. Cesmat was ninety-three years of age when he died at Bakersfield. A pioneering spirit had prompted him to leave his homeland for a hoped-for better life, and he experienced both the joys and the sufferings which often characterized the life of the French in the United States.

The Brown House, one of Delano's first hotels, circa 1889. Left to right: Edward Shilling, Hortensia Mandis, Ulysses Mandis, Frances Mandis (wife of Adrien), Sam Shilling, Rita Shilling (sister of Frances), and "Alerena" Nellie Mandis. (Photo courtesy of John Crawford)

Jean Adrien Mandis, one of Delano's first French residents. (Photo courtesy of John Crawford)

French Settlers Of North Kern

The 1887 wedding picture of Ambroise Villard and Eugénie Faure. (Photo courtesy of Anne Villard Blanc)

The Villard family in 1905. Back row: Eugène, Ambroise, Adrienne, Eugénie, Albert (in back of mother), August and Joseph. Front row: Jule, Mary, and Gabriel. (Photo courtesy of Anne Villard Blanc)

The Villard ranch in Rag Gulch, circa 1920. (Photo courtesy of Anne Villard Blanc)

The Faure Brothers' General Merchandise Store on High Street in Delano with André Vieux (second from right). (Photo courtesy of Pete Rostain.)

Inside André Vieux's store after 1909, with Joe Vial (behind counter), Mrs. Stokes and her son Johnny, and Anaïs (Rostain) Vieux. (Photo courtesy of Pete Rostain.)

The Perriers' saloon with rooms to let in the back. The sign advertises latrines, liquors and cigars. (Photo courtesy of Pete Rostain)

Annie, Auguste and Angéline Perrier. (Photo courtesy of Auguste Dusserre)

Auguste and Paulin Dusserre with the venerable Joseph Perrier. (Photo courtesy of Auguste Dusserre)

The Delano Hotel built by Auguste Borel. (Photo courtesy of the Delano Historical Society)

Four French brides of early Delano: Louise (Borel) Escallier (later Faure), Anaïs (Villard) Rostain (later Vieux), Marie (Labarthe) Borel, and Anaïs (Escallier) Eustache. (Photo courtesy of Louise Borel Panero)

The children of Auguste and Marie (Labarthe) Borel: Martha, Ernest, Louise, and Angèle. (Photo courtesy of Louise Borel Panero)

Two pioneer hotelmen of Delano, Léon and Antoine Escallier. (Photo courtesy of Louise Borel Panero)

Léon Escallier with his bride, Louise Borel, later the wife of Pierre Faure. (Photo courtesy of Louise Borel Panero)

French Settlers Of North Kerr

Pierre Faure and his bride, the former Louise (Borel) Escallier. (Photo courtesy of Louise Borel Panero)

Lest We Forget

The former Ida Moreau and her husband Jules Escallier. (Photo courtesy of Catherine Castagnet Richaud)

The predominantly French Catholic community of Delano in 1910, in front of St. Mary's Church at 12th and Main Streets.

The Reynaud home in Delano, circa 1910, with Marcel and Hortense Reynaud, their daughters Marcelle and Blanche, and Mary and Victor Seinturier. (Photo courtesy of Marcelle Reynaud Borel)

After the baptism of baby Marcelle with the proud parents, Hortense and Marcel Reynaud, and godparents, Annie Rostain and Victor Seinturier. (Photo courtesy of Marcelle Reynaud Borel)

The Pioneer Saloon in Famoso in 1919 with Clementine Orcier and Edna Overton. (Photo courtesy of Clementine Orcier Johnson)

Joseph Bertrand plying his trade as a cobbler in Delano. (Photo courtesy of the Delano Historical Society)

Lest We Forget

Another of the many French marriages made in Kern. The 1903 wedding photo of Marie Mélanie Morel and Romulus Orcier. (Photo courtesy of Julia Morel Overton)

Joseph Cesmat, at the age of ninety-three, enjoying retirement at the home of his son Jules. (Photo courtesy of Jules Cesmat)

CHAPTER VIII

East Bakersfield: Heart Of The French Colony

For many decades East Bakersfield was foremost among Kern County's communities with a business and social orientation that was uniquely French. Construction on the Southern Pacific was approaching Bakersfield in 1874 when that town's fathers refused to make certain concessions that were requested by the railroad officials. Consequently the company laid out its own town about a mile east of Bakersfield in the fall and named it Sumner, after Senator Charles Sumner of Massachusetts. Understandably concerned over the placing of this rival settlement so near at hand, the editor of the Bakersfield *Kern County Courier* declared that the new town was "not needed."

Nonetheless rival Sumner became a busy railroad town replete with its depot, roundhouse, switching yard, and livestock pens, as well as nearby sheep shearing facilities. By early 1876 several stores, hotels, and restaurants had been established on I Street (later renamed Sumner Street), and the *Kern County Gazette* envisaged a "place of great importance." In 1893 the bustling town was incorporated with a new name, becoming Kern City. Subsequently Bakersfield became a thriving oil town early in the twentieth century, and it was about twice the size of its rival when Kern City was annexed in 1909, and by geographical designation it became East Bakersfield.

The outstanding pioneer businessman of the town that became East Bakersfield was Victor Louis Amy, called by a contemporary the "French Giant of Sumner."* His father, Claude Benoît Amy, the son of a well-to-do silk merchant of Lyon,

---

* Gratefully acknowledged is the genealogical help of Camille Zimmerman, a great-grandniece of Victor L. Amy.

France, had married a working girl, Victoire Julie Deboissy, and his disapproving parents relegated him to far flung branches of the family business. Consequently his children were born in various parts of France and Germany. Victor L. Amy was born in Paris, and at the age of sixteen he joined the rush of "forty-niners" to the fabled gold fields of California. There he soon found that trading was more profitable than mining and so he became a businessman. In 1851 he invited his parents, together with his brothers and sisters, to come to California, and they sailed aboard the Courrier de l'Inde. Seven months later, after a harrowing voyage around Cape Horn, they reached San Francisco.

The city by the Golden Gate dismayed the newly-arrived family of Claude B. Amy. Daughter Amanda married François H. Parent, a French merchant. When her baby was born she feared it might die of cholera and persuaded her husband to take her to France, where after an arduous trip the baby died, as did also the broken-hearted mother. In the meantime the Amy family had moved to Sonora, in the Sierra Nevada, where they settled on a ranch and lived among stately linden trees. Daughter Eugénie married Edward Keil, a Bavarian, which was an uncomfortable union at the time of the Franco-Prussian War. Son Léon became an actor and toured the mining camps until his death at Curtis Creek in 1872. Daughter Mathilde married a Belgian, Félix Désiré Duquesne, and for a time they lived at Sumner, but then they left to become pioneer hotelkeepers at Fresno. Son Melchior, who was a frequent visitor at Sumner, suffered from poor health, and while visiting France was killed by a train in 1909.

Beginning with his business activities during the gold rush, Victor L. Amy, somewhat of a bon vivant who never married, fared better than any other member of his family. While Amy was a merchant and hotelman at Hornitos and Bear Valley in Mariposa County, he became associated with Beneditto Ardizzi, an Italian Swiss. Successively they continued their business association at Snelling in Merced County, and at Delano and Sumner in Kern County.

East Bakersfield: Heart Of The French Colony

The Amy and Ardizzi mercantile firm at Sumner was organized as a legal partnership on Bastille Day, 1876, and quickly became a headquarters for the sheepmen, as well as the itinerant herders, of Kern County. While carrying them on their books the merchants shared their economic ups and downs over the years. The Amy and Ardizzi partnership prospered in proportion to the economic growth of Sumner. Amy was appointed the first postmaster of the town in mid-1876, and in that same year he became a member of the Kern County Democratic Central Committee.

Kern County journalists delighted in referring to Victor L. Amy as a "large proprietor," which in a serious vein was related to the size of his business but in a jocular one was a poke at his great girth. When he went to Paso Robles Springs "for the benefit of his health" in the summer of 1877, the editor of the *Kern County Gazette* expressed the hope that he would "return as sound as a dollar, as slim as a rail, and as active as a cat." Yet when he returned from a buying trip to San Francisco and a visit with his relatives at Sonora, reportedly he was "only eighteen pounds heavier than when he left home."

Because of his deteriorating health, Amy was under treatment in San Francisco at the French Hospital, of which he was a director, when he died in the summer of 1881.* His obituary appeared in San Francisco newspapers, as well as those of Mariposa and Kern Counties. The six-foot "Sumner giant" at the time of his death weighed four hundred and two pounds, and presumably he had smothered in his own fat. His remains were interred in the family plot at Sonora. In his will he had provided that the firm of Amy and Ardizzi should remain intact until mid-1884, at which time his property was divided among his heirs.

Beneditto Ardizzi subsequently enlisted as a new associate Louis Virgin Olcese, an Italian American son of argonaut friends, and they became partners in the firm of Ardizzi-Olcese.

---

* The French Hospital was sponsored by a benevolent association to which many of Kern County's French belonged.

Lest We Forget

Olcese was fluent in several languages, including French, which he spoke so well that he was readily accepted as a compatriot by the French of East Bakersfield. With the coming of hard times in the early 1890s, the firm of Ardizzi-Olcese had to declare bankruptcy. Soon after the embittered Ardizzi had signed the necessary papers, he died an insolvent debtor in mid-1895. While recovering from this setback the firm necessarily foreclosed on long overdue debts of sheepmen, yet few of his contemporaries ever spoke ill of Olcese.

By the 1890s the Ardizzi-Olcese firm was handling large amounts of money and its scrip was readily accepted in the San Joaquin Valley. In 1918 the federal government required that the firm, in light of its bank-like activities, organize the Ardizzi-Olcese Bank, which was known locally as the Alley Bank. After being absorbed into the Bank of Italy, it became the East Bakersfield branch of the Bank of America. In the meantime Louis V. Olcese had died in mid-1929, and the Ardizzi-Olcese firm went out of business early in 1930.

Arsène Peter Bernard, a prominent French citizen of East Bakersfield, was a native of the Lake Ponchartrain area of Louisiana. After graduating from a Jesuit college in St. Louis, Missouri, this heir to a family fortune and his bride Elzira went to Rusk, Texas, where Bernard opened a general merchandise store in the early 1850s. Later in that decade he joined William Walker's ill-fated filibustering expedition to Nicaragua. Bernard's filibustering days were over when he became a businessman at Vacaville, in northern California. While there he helped in the building of the Vaca Valley Railroad, which linked Vacaville and Elmira in 1869.

Upon becoming enthusiastic about the developing San Joaquin Valley, Arsène P. Bernard moved to Kern County in 1874 and settled at Sumner, and began to acquire a substantial amount of land on the north side of the town. Early in 1875, a few months after the Southern Pacific had reached Sumner, he placed an omnibus in service between the railroad station and the hotels of Bakersfield. After being appointed Kern County Treasurer in 1879, he was elected to that office in 1880, 1882,

East Bakersfield: Heart Of The French Colony

and 1884. For his private tutoring of French grateful students gave him an inscribed silver pitcher, which became a cherished family heirloom. When he died in mid-1891, his widow went into mourning and wore black for the next eighteen years.

Upon the death of his father, James A. Bernard, a native of Rusk, Texas, left railroad employment in order to administer his father's estate. This involved the subdividing of a quarter section of land through which ran Arsene and Elzira Streets, which were named after James's parents and subsequently renamed Jefferson and Lincoln Streets. Within the subdivision the family name has been retained for Bernard Street. He married Edith (Maggie) Long, the sixteen-year-old daughter of family friends, in 1876. They became the parents of seven children, the oldest of whom, Clophine, studied nursing at the French Hospital and married Dr. Carlos White of Tulare County. When Kern City was incorporated in 1893, Bernard became one of the town's first trustees. About the time that Kern City was annexed to Bakersfield, in 1909, Bernard moved his family to what had been a summer home at Ocean Park. He was on one of his occasional business trips to Bakersfield when he died at the Metropole Hotel in mid-1916.

Yet another of East Bakersfield's prominent French businessmen was Jean B. Estribou, a native of Ogeu in the Lower Pyrenees. In 1895, two years after his arrival in Kern County, he established the Metropole Market on Baker Street. In addition to his store he had a ranch a few miles southeast of Bakersfield where he raised cattle and alfalfa, as well as operated a slaughterhouse. The children who visited his market, whether they were on an errand for their mothers or not, knew that kind Estribou was always "good for a free wiener."

Edouard Lafontaine was one of Sumner's pioneer hotelmen, and in the summer of 1876 he advertised in the *Kern County Gazette* the opening of his French Hotel and Restaurant, which were on G Street (later renamed 19th Street). Near the end of that year the hotel was enlarged in order "to accommodate his friends." In addition to the "particular care" Lafontaine afforded his patrons, he also operated a "feed yard" for the benefit of their horses. Several years later, when he was no longer a hotelman but rather a stage driver on the route between Sumner and Linn's Valley, the Bakersfield *Californian* reported that Lafontaine had bought the stage line in 1891.

More than any other street in East Bakersfield, Humboldt (originally named H Street and then successively renamed Humboldt Street and 21st Street) long was the main artery through the French quarter. Along it were many French-owned businesses, among them the French House and Livery Stable, owned by Jean Cesmat, one of the pioneer Alpine Frenchmen of the town. A native of Manse, he arrived in America in search of his fortune in 1859. Besides the hotel he also owned considerable sheep and land in Kern County. When Cesmat died in 1885, his estate went to a younger brother, Marius, who had come to Kern County in 1874. In the same year that his older brother died, Marius and his wife Eliza (Roquette) lost an infant son, and she in turn died four years later. In 1890 he married Frances Mouliot.

In the summer of 1898 an arsonist-caused fire consumed nearly the entire business section of East Bakersfield, and caused the death of Joseph Gallien, an employee of the stable owned by Eugène Verdier. The majority of the burned structures were owned by Frenchmen, and they soon set about rebuilding their businesses. Where the original French House had stood on Humboldt Street, Marius Cesmat built with brick the Cesmat Hotel. During this period of rebuilding a new French House was constructed across the street from the Cesmat Hotel by Marius Plantier. A native of Orcières in the Upper Alps, he had come to Kern County in 1881, worked as a baker, and married his employer's half sister, Marie Espitallier. At the corner of Humboldt and Baker Streets was the Gap Hotel, owned by François Espitallier, a native a Ancelle in the Upper Alps. His wife Anaïs (Philipp), a native of the Alpine town of Gap, died while giving birth to her second child, which led Espitallier to leave the hotel business for sheep raising. The Gap Hotel was owned by Eugène Verdier when it burned in the fire of mid-1898. Unlike many of his neighbors, Verdier was a native of

East Bakersfield: Heart Of The French Colony

Gers in southwestern France. A few years after the fire he built the Imperial Hotel at the corner of Humboldt and Baker Streets. In 1908 he leased the hotel to a trio of Alpine Frenchmen—Léon Abonel, Pierre Raymond, and Jean Zampa—and he and his wife Marie (Laborde) moved to Granite Station. Another hotel built after the fire was the National, located at the corner of Humboldt and Kern Streets. Its builders were Pierre and Bernard Sartiat, natives of the Lower Pyrenees, who had prospered as ranchers in the Tehachapi Mountains. Later they moved their business next door to the French House, at the corner of Humboldt and Baker Streets. Subsequently the hotel was owned by Justin and Julie (Rambaud) Borel. Another post-fire hotel was the Universal, built at the corner of Humboldt and Baker Streets by Jean Philipp, a pioneer sheepman of Kern County. It replaced a rooming house and saloon at the site previously run by Philipp and his older partner, Jacques Dusserre. The Universal Hotel had changed hands several times before it was acquired by Martin Jaussaud, and long after many of East Bakersfield's erstwhile French-owned hotels had been acquired by Basques the Universal remained in French hands. It had a reputation for lively card games, savory meals, and perennial herders looking for a game of bocces.

Among the numerous saloonkeepers of East Bakersfield was Jean Eyraud, a native of La Motte in the Upper Alps, who came to Kern County in 1880, where he was a sheepman for several years before entering business. In 1883, while Eyraud was a sheepman he guided a Chicago scientist to the top of Mount Whitney, earning $500 for ten days of service, and on top of that mountain he drank his first champagne since coming to the United States. In 1887 he married Constance Marin, a native of the Upper Alps, and soon after that he went into business at a site opposite the railroad depot. His place of business was known later as the New Commercial.

Although Marius Martin Espitallier was not East Bakersfield's first baker, he was in that business by the late 1880s. He was a native of Ancelle in the Upper Alps who had reached San Francisco in 1874, following the baking trade there and at San

Lest We Forget

Jose before coming to Kern County. In 1887 he married Appolonie Eyraud and acquired the French Bakery on Humboldt Street. The townsfolk called Appolonie the "Morning Echo," for, like the newspaper of that name, she was always first with the news. After the fire of mid-1898 Espitallier built again, constructing this time a brick building which housed a curious combination of bakery and saloon. At that time good French bread sold for six cents a loaf in a transaction that could be made with octagonal brass tokens that bore on one side the name of the bakery, its owner, and the value, and on the other "good for one loaf of bread."

Especially in the early years of its existence the French Bakery frequently changed hands. Joe Bresson took it over briefly and then in turn sold it to Augustin Amour who, in 1912, built a new bakery next door to the old one. With an added second story the old building under its new owner, Joseph Espitallier, became the Hôtel des Alpes. For a time Marcel Reynaud and Joseph Gueyden were partners of Amour in the operation of the French Bakery, but in 1918 Gueyden became the sole owner. For him and his wife Léa (Marin) the bakery building was both a place of business and a family residence for many years. In the mid-1940s Pierre Laxague purchased the French Bakery, and as the ownership went from French to French Basque the name was changed to the Pyrenees Bakery. Many local bakers had been apprentices at the French Bakery.

Long engaged in the baking business in East Bakersfield was the Galland family, beginning with Jean Galland, a native of the Upper Alps, who started his career at the Parisian Bakery in Bakersfield. Subsequently he worked at virtually all of the bakeries on the west and east sides of town, and his descendants continued to ply the trade at Galland's Bakery on East 18th Street.

Of more short-lived fame was the California Bakery owned and operated by a Béarnais couple, Auguste and Anna Cazassus. After selling out in 1904, the couple moved to Bishop where they opened a French laundry. Among the great attractions of

East Bakersfield: Heart Of The French Colony

their business, popular with local French herders, were the "first class thirty-five cent baths."

East Bakersfield had its share of French blacksmiths, among them Théophile Isnard, a native of the Upper Alps, who found his way to Kern County. He established his shop at the busy intersection of Baker and East 19th Streets. Soon after he had entered business he married Léa Bonhomme, and they lived at the rear of his shop. He invented a sheep's foot or earth tamper and applied for a patent, only to find that someone else had been granted one on the device. A few years after Isnard's death from tuberculosis his widow married Jean Barthélemy, one of the many French sheepmen of Kern County. After being left a widow for the second time, Léa supported herself and her children by working as a midwife in East Bakersfield. Prosper Paquette, a French Canadian, was another of East Bakersfield's blacksmiths. His shop was conveniently close by Cesmat's Livery Stable on Humboldt Street. When Paquette died in 1911, his blacksmithing business was purchased by Bernard Uhalt, a native of Pau in the Basque country.

Along Humboldt Street (later renamed East 21st Street) were the homes of several French families of East Bakersfield. Among them was that of Jean B. Estribou and his wife Sophie (Laborde), both natives of the Lower Pyrenees. The merchant's brick house cost $3,000, which was a considerable amount at the time it was built. Nearby was the home of François Provensal and his wife Félicie (Bonhomme), who were natives of the Upper Alps. He was engaged in borax mining in the vicinity of Frazier Park. Two of the French families that lived on Humboldt Street had the same name—Raymond—but were not related. One was that of Jean A. Raymond and his wife Rose (Eyraud), both of them natives of the Upper Alps. He was engaged in sheep raising, having come to Kern County to join his father, bringing with him his mother, his brother Pierre, his sister Louise, who married Eli Blanc, and Rose, who married Vincent Rambaud. In a nearby residence lived Jean B. Raymond and his wife Marie (Galvin). As a sheepman, he was known by the distinguishing sobriquet "Famoso," which he had earned as a herder in his younger days at Delano. Elie Matheron and his wife Alphonsine (Marin), both natives of the Upper Alps, lived for a few years on a ranch in the Tehachapi Valley before they moved to a stately house on Humboldt Street. Living nearby on that street were Jean Pourroy and his wife Emilie (Villard), also natives of the Upper Alps. After being active as a sheepman near Delano, Pourroy engaged in farming near Bakersfield.

More than any other place in Kern County, East Bakersfield was the heart of the French colony between about 1880 and 1920. Compatriots living in outlying areas maintained close economic and cultural ties with its residents. Through marriages many of its families became related to others throughout the county, and over the years there was an influx of families from nearby areas. The distinctive French atmosphere in East Bakersfield was long preserved by the continued use of the language, celebration of traditional festivities, and prevailing membership in the Catholic Church.

In addition to the original marriages among the French that brought about extended family relationships in Kern County, the same trend developed from the subsequent marriages of widowers and widows. In cases of the death of one or both parents, relatives often took care of the surviving children. Yet, as an old timer stated, "there were an awful lot of dogies in those days." Some French children lived for varying lengths of time at the Children's Shelter, which was located in a building that later housed the Sinaloa Restaurant. The three small children of Alexandre and Marceline (Lacoste) Abadie—Franklin, George, and Jeanne—for a time after their mother's death in 1913 lived in the orphanage until the father could care for them himself.

Among the popular fraternal organizations of East Bakersfield was the Sumner Grove, No. 56, Ancient Order of Druids, which was instituted in the spring of 1886, with a roster of thirty-four charter members. The predominantly French and Italian membership had nearly doubled by 1894, and the participants long remembered the family picnics sponsored by the Druids at the Tejon Ranch, in the Tehachapi Mountains.

East Bakersfield: Heart Of The French Colony

The same eroding historical forces at work in the 1920s dissolving the social fabric of the French colony of East Bakersfield at the same time were obliterating the French landmarks of the community. Only a few lingering traces of the once thriving French quarter of what was successively Sumner, Kern City, and East Bakersfield remained by the 1970s.

The Ardizzi-Olcese Company, formerly Amy and Ardizzi, on Sumner Street. East Bakersfield's oldest general store.

Claude Benoît Amy. He brought his family around the Horn to a new life in California's gold country. (Photo courtesy of Camille Zimmerman)

Victoire Julie (Deboissy) Amy. Her husband's family frowned on her marriage to Claude. (Photo courtesy of Camille Zimmerman)

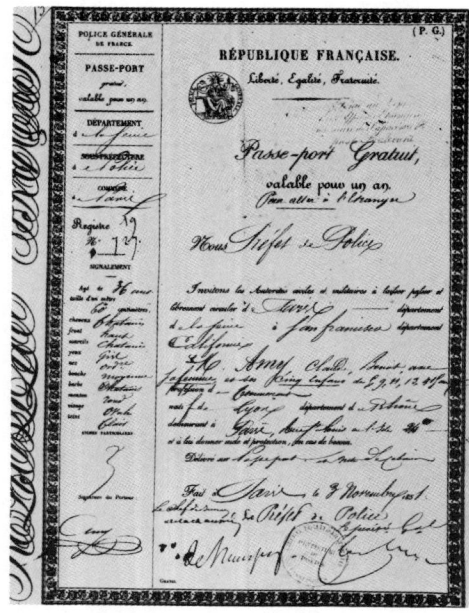

The Amy family passport issued on November 3, 1851. (Document courtesy of Camille Zimmerman)

Mathilde (Amy) Duquesne. She and her husband moved from Sumner to Fresno after the death of her older brother Victor. (Photo courtesy of Camille Zimmerman)

Félix Désiré Duquesne worked as a bookkeeper for Amy and Ardizzi. (Photo courtesy of Camille Zimmerman)

Beneditto Ardizzi died an insolvent debtor. (Photo courtesy of the Kern County Museum)

Louis Virgin Olcese replaced Victor Louis Amy in the firm of Amy and Ardizzi. (Photo courtesy of Thelma De Pauli Campbell)

Inscribed in French, Victor Louis Amy's tombstone stands watch over his 740 pound bronze casket buried in the family plot at the Masonic Cemetery in Sonora, California.

Lest We Forget

The Ardizzi-Olcese scrip was as good as gold throughout the entire San Joaquin Valley. (Scrip courtesy of Everett Sterner)

Louis Olcese bankrolled the sheepmen in good times and bad. (Photo courtesy of Henry Blanc)

Arsène Peter Bernard believed that California's promise lay in the agricultural lands of the San Joaquin Valley. (Photo courtesy of Carleen White Phelan)

Elzira Bernard went into mourning for twelve years following the death of her husband in 1891. (Photo courtesy of Carleen White Phelan)

Inside the Bernard family home on Sumner Street in 1910 when Amelia (Mouliot) and Arsene Reed Bernard lived there. (Photo courtesy of Minnie Guhl Cesmat)

Corrennah and James A. Bernard Jr. in front of the family home on Sumner Street. (Photo courtesy of Carleen White Phelan)

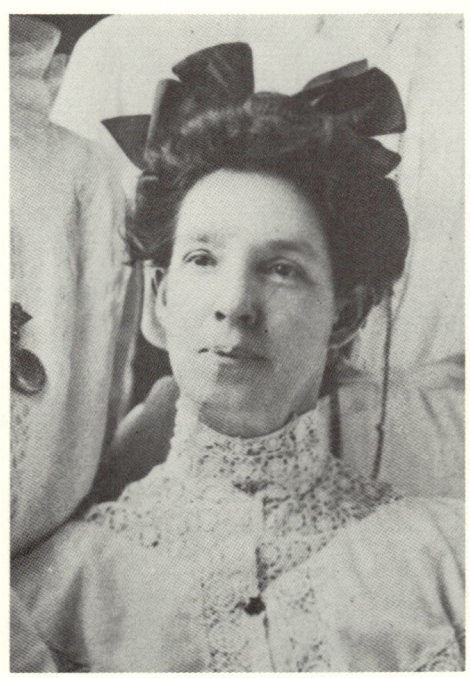

Edith "Maggie" Long married James A. Bernard at the age of sixteen. (Photo courtesy of Carleen White Phelan)

Clophine Bernard trained as a nurse at the French Hospital in San Francisco. Returning from vacation, she received a pass from the governor to go back to San Francisco following the earthquake in 1906. (Photo courtesy of Carleen White Phelan)

James A. Bernard with his granddaughter Carleen White. (Photo courtesy of Carleen White Phelan)

Inside the Metropole Meat Market with its proprietor Jean Estribou on the left. (Photo courtesy of Denise Estribou Sherman)

Sumner's first French House was destroyed in the fire of 1898. Far left: Marius Espitallier. Center, holding a turkey on a cue stick: Marius Cesmat, proprietor. Far right: Prosper Paquette, blacksmith. Photo circa 1892. (Photo courtesy of Minnie Guhl Cesmat)

The Cesmat Stables, circa 1892. On horseback at far left: Faustino Noriega. Rider on right: Marius Cesmat. (Photo courtesy of Minnie Guhl Cesmat)

A group of Frenchmen playing boules or "bocces" on the lot between Plantier's French House and Prosper Paquette's blacksmith shop, circa 1910. Left to right: Unknown, Jean "La Motte" Eyraud, Marius Plantier, Frank "Passoir" Philippe, Eli Blanc, Auguste Pierre Eyraud, Madeleine Borel, two unknowns, Auguste Maurel, Marius Martin Espitallier, Romulus Borel, Pierre "Pete" Lambert, Jean B. "Famoso" Raymond, Pierre "de l'ours" Faure. Note pigeonholes on barn. (Photo courtesy of Jeanne Abadie Edmondson)

Jean Baptiste Bergès, Marius Cesmat, Frances and Laura Mouliot, on September 13, 1890. If Jean Baptiste had had his way, it would have been a double wedding. However, two months later he married Marie Inda. (Photo courtesy of Minnie Guhl Cesmat)

Marius Cesmat came to Kern County in 1874 to work as a sheepherder for his older brother Jean. (Photo courtesy of Minnie Guhl Cesmat)

The Cesmat family in 1894 with Charles, Marius, Frances and baby Marius who died two years later. (Photo courtesy of Minnie Guhl Cesmat)

The Cesmat Hotel, rebuilt after the fire of 1898 on the site of the original French House, with Marius Cesmat on the far left. Years later the hotel came to be known as the Amestoy. (Photo courtesy of Minnie Guhl Cesmat)

Plantier's French House, later known as the Basque Cafe, at 631 E. 21st Street, in 1900. Left to right: Marie (Espitallier) Plantier, baby Agnes Plantier, Marie Louise Allemand, Lucille Pellisson, Marie Louise Nouguier, Marius Plantier, and an unknown. (Photo courtesy of Agnes Plantier Wilton)

The wedding picture of Marie Espitallier and Marius Plantier taken in the late 1890s.

Madeleine Borel and Joseph Bresson standing in front of the entrance to the French House, circa 1909. (Photo courtesy of the Borel descendants)

Lest We Forget

The wedding photo of François Etienne Espitallier and Anaïs Philipp, sister of pioneer hotelman Jean Philipp. (Photo courtesy of Etienne Espitallier)

The National Hotel, on the corner of Kern and Humboldt Streets, owned by the Sartiat brothers. Front row, left to right: Pierre Sartiat, Marie Louise (Richaud) Sartiat, Marceline Lacoste. The man on the far right is gesturing to a group of men playing bocces to stay out of the picture. (Photo courtesy of Jeanne Abadie Edmondson)

The National Hotel at its new location on the corner of Humboldt and Baker Streets. The man with his hand on the carriage wheel is Zéphirin Boisseranc. (Photo courtesy of Dorita Boisseranc Iacopetti)

The Boisseranc wedding party in 1911. Back seat: Louise (Richaud) Burgemaster, Zéphirin Boisseranc and his bride, Louise Bernard-Raymond. In the front seat: Bernard Pierre Sartiat and his father Pierre. (Photo courtesy of Dorita Boisseranc Iacopetti)

Justin Borel and his wife, the former Julie Rambaud, took over the National Hotel from the Sartiats. (Photo courtesy of Yvonne Borel Curran)

The Jaussaud family, Ermance, Dermide "Babe" Martin Jr., and Martin Sr., at the Belle Vue Ranch, as it was known, in 1921. (Photo courtesy of the Aubin family)

The Universal Hotel, rebuilt in 1902 after the fire by Jean Philipp. Holding the bocces: Jean Seinturier. To the far right: Jean Philipp and Auguste Maurel. (Photo courtesy of Eleanor Johnson Wells)

Outside the Universal Hotel, circa 1910. Left to right: three unknown men, Marie Garnier, Emily Baum, Marie Roux, Marie Louise Philipp with Jeannette, Louise (Philipp) Roux with Irene, Lydia Bécaïs, later the wife of Léon Abonel. (Photo courtesy of Marie Roux Hardwick)

Inside the Universal Hotel which housed the last of the old-style French restaurants in East Bakersfield. At the head of the table and clockwise: Martin Jaussaud Sr., Emile Oddous, two unknowns, Emile Jaussaud (no relation), Martin Jaussaud Jr., two unknowns, Baptiste Oddous, Jules Garnier.

Inside Jean Eyraud's New Commercial Saloon on Sumner Street. Mustachioed barman is Emile Chevalier. At the cash register is Pete Chabre. (Photo courtesy of Helen Chevalier Johnson)

Jean "La Motte" Eyraud guided a climber to the top of Mount Whitney in 1883 and then tasted his first champagne since leaving France. (Photo courtesy of Constance Eyraud Apperson)

Jean Eyraud's saloon facing the railroad depot on Sumner Street. (Photo courtesy of Constance Eyraud Apperson)

Lest We Forget

Appolonie Eyraud and Marius Martin Espitallier were married in Kern County in 1887. Her right hand rests on the photo album belonging to the Romulus Borel family.

The Kern City Bakery and Saloon on Humboldt Street (later East 21st), owned first by Marius Martin Espitallier. Taken over in 1910 by Joseph Espitallier, a story was added to the building and it became the Hôtel des Alpes. The men standing left to right: Germain Vivian, "Gros" Jean Espitallier, _____ Julien, and Henri Espitallier. (Photo courtesy of Louise Espitallier Kuhs)

The Kern City Pyrenees Bakery with its new owner, Pierre Laxague, in 1947 before it was moved to Pioneer Village at the Kern County Museum. (Photo courtesy of Dermide Jaussaud)

Front and back of an octagonal brass token used by the Kern City Bakery. (Token courtesy of Pierre Laxague)

The Galland and Viau families. Left to right, top row: Ludovic Galland, Josephine Viau, Ada Viau, Elysée Galland. Bottom row: Blanche (on mother's lap), Alexina, Alta, Jean, Buster, Grandmother and Grandfather Viau. (Photo courtesy of Blanche Galland Carter)

Joseph Gueydan, long-time owner of the French Bakery, with Pierre "Pete" Laborde.

Augustin Amour built a new bakery at 717 Humboldt Street in 1912. (Photo courtesy of Linda Amour)

Inside the old Kern City Bakery. Right to left: Pierre Jean "Pete" Aubin, Augustin Amour, Leon Eyraud, and Jim Hamilton. (Photo courtesy of Mary Abonel)

The California Bakery on G Street (later East 19th) with owners Auguste and Anna Cazassus. The small sign above the window reads: "This shop open again. Will give 35 loaves for $1." (Photo courtesy of Bertha Berges Gates)

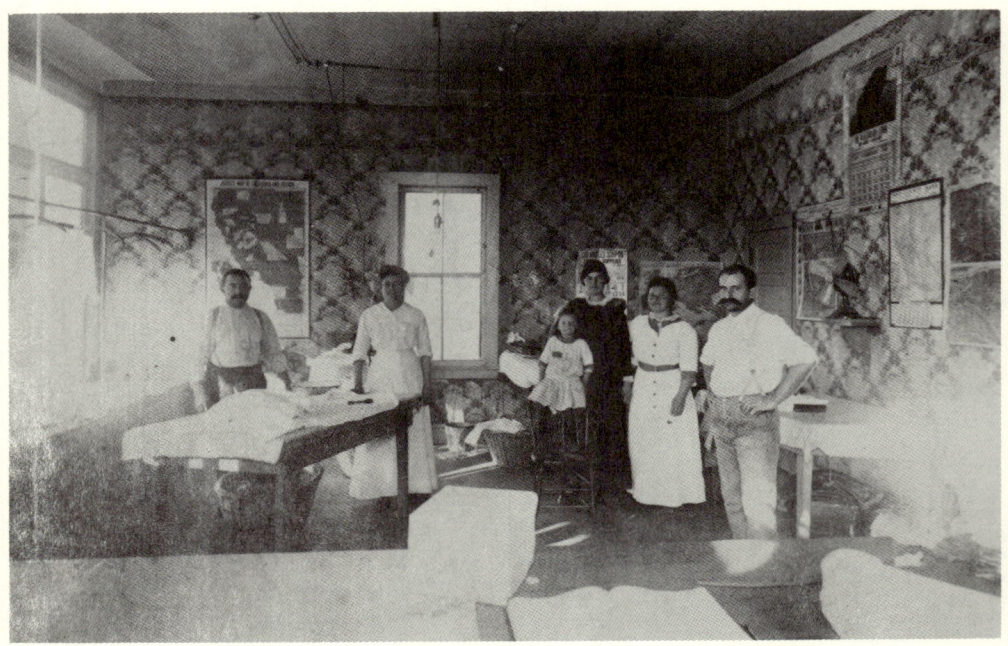

The French Laundry in Bishop advertising first class baths for thirty-five cents. Left to right: Léon Orcier, _____ Arzul, unknown, Jacques Bayes, Auguste and Anna Cazassus, and an unknown. (Photo courtesy of Bertha Bergès Gates)

Inside the French Laundry in Bishop, in 1914. Left to right: Auguste and Anna Cazassus, Bertha Bergès, two employees and a friend. (Photo courtesy of Bertha Bergès Gates)

Bernard Uhalt (on right), new owner of Prosper Paquette's blacksmith shop on Humboldt, circa 1911. (Photo courtesy of Pete and Gina Uhalt)

Pete Rambaud, a second generation French sheepherder, following in the footsteps of his father Vincent Rambaud. Far from being undesirable, the black sheep were used as markers to facilitate the counting of the flock. (Photo courtesy of Jennie Rambaud)

Théophile Isnard, second man from right, with his sheep's foot or earth tamper for which he was seeking a patent. (Photo courtesy of Winifred Barthélemy Sasia)

Seated are Théophile Isnard and his bride Léa Bonhomme. Standing are Virginia (Blanc) Chabre and Silvio Selna, guard for the Ardizzi-Olcese Company. (Photo courtesy of Winifred Barthélemy Sasia)

A Barthélemy family portrait. Left to right: Winifred, Léa holding Francine, Jean and Leon. (Photo courtesy of Leah Provensal Castro)

East Bakersfield: Heart Of The French Colony

The Provensal family, left to right: Félix, Félicie (Bonhomme) Provensal holding Frank Jr., Leah, and François. (Photo courtesy of Leah Provensal Castro)

Frank Provensal with his son Félix at a borax mine near Frazier Park, circa 1907. (Photo courtesy of Leah Provensal Castro)

The wedding photo of Eli Blanc and Louise Raymond, married October 28, 1901. (Photo courtesy of Anne Villard Blanc)

The Estribou family home on Humboldt Street. Left to right: Denise, Sophie (Laborde) Estribou, Paul, Alfred and Frank. (Photo courtesy of Leah Provensal Castro)

The Jean B. Raymond residence at 518 Humboldt Street. Standing on porch: Marie (Galvin) Raymond holding son Jean Jr. with her daughter Bertha. (Photo courtesy of Jeanette Galland Collins)

The Jean A. Raymond family. Left to right: Jean A. Raymond Sr., Jean Jr., Marcelle, Rose (Eyraud) Raymond holding Denise. (Photo courtesy of Leah Provensal Castro)

The Elie Matheron family, left to right, Blanche, Elie, Henry, Alphonsine, and Emile. (Photo courtesy of Marcelle Reynaud Borel)

The Matheron residence at 325 Humboldt Street in 1910. Left to right: Alphonsine (Marin) Matheron, Elie Matheron, Baptiste Oddous, Henry and Emile Matheron. (Photo courtesy of Marcelle Reynaud Borel)

A photo taken at the baptism of Valentin Vivian. Standing: Valentin Lafont and Célestin Vivian. Seated: Marie (Achin) Lafont, baby Valentin Vivian and Lydie (Eyraud) Vivian. (Photo courtesy of Leah Provensal Castro)

Marceline Lacoste and Alexandre Abadie, married July 9, 1904. (Photo courtesy of Jeanne Abadie Edmondson)

CHAPTER IX

Tehachapi: Little Béarn

Tehachapi, an Indian name, has been given to a mountain range, mountain pass, and mountain valley within Kern County. Many authors have been fascinated by the train trip up winding Tehachapi Pass, including Benjamin F. Taylor who described the experience in a book entitled *Between the Gates*. During the climb the train circled through "a mob of mountain peaks," which, he observed, "disputed the right of way." In mid-1876, after several months of heavy construction, the Southern Pacific's rails had been laid to the Tehachapi Valley where the company founded Summit Station. Around it developed the town of Tehachapi, while at the same time an older settlement at the west end of the valley, known as Williamsburg, declined in importance, becoming known as Old Town.

As was often the case with newly-founded railroad towns, Tehachapi's pioneer businessmen built stores, hotels, restaurants, and saloons along a single street that ran parallel to the tracks, which the subdividers named G Street. Subsequently it was renamed Tehachapi Boulevard. Among the town's pioneer businessmen was a Frenchman, Victor Bresson, who in the late 1880s built the French Hotel. The hotel building was destroyed by fire in 1896, and he sold the lot and returned to France. Some two years later an old barn was moved to the site, and after undergoing appropriate remodeling it became the Eagle Hotel. Whether its proprietor was a Frenchman is problematical, but the meals were prepared in the French style. In 1900 the hotel was purchased by John Iribarne, an American-born Basque, who renamed it El Nido and continued to serve French cuisine. By then the town's Alpine French hotelmen were being replaced by Béarnais compatriots from the Lower Pyrenees, as well as by the Basques.

The Tehachapi Hotel, which was opened in 1903, was housed in a former schoolhouse. Louis Vidaillet bought the building from Frank Dufour, a retired cattleman, and moved it to the corner of F and Green Streets. The Tehachapi Hotel underwent several changes in ownership before it was bought by François Bernard in 1908. He and his wife Marie (Pellisson) were natives of the Upper Alps. Her brother Joseph Pellisson became the bartender, and the Tehachapi Hotel became a favorite gathering place for the French of Tehachapi Valley. After the death of her husband in 1941, Marie Bernard sold the business and bought the Basko Hotel on the opposite side of the railroad tracks. It had been built by George Esponda in 1896 and was the property of various French and Basque proprietors, including Jack Iriart and his brother-in-law Gus Cazacus, before being taken over by Marie Bernard.

Another of Tehachapi's French-owned hotels was the Commercial, built by Marius Cesmat in about 1900 on G Street (renamed Tehachapi Boulevard). Cesmat was an East Bakersfield hotelman, and the management of the Commercial Hotel was entrusted to Pierre Laffargue, a native of the Lower Pyrenees, whose wife Marie (Martinto) was a French Basque. After her death Laffargue, while on a visit to the place of his birth, married Madeleine Fillet and brought her to Kern County. She was lonely in the unfamiliar surroundings of Tehachapi and sent for her sister Anna, who in 1905 married Jean Baptiste Capdeville, who also was a native of the Lower Pyrenees. The Capdevilles opened a rooming house in Tehachapi.

In the course of changing ownership the Commercial Hotel was bought by Cyrille Giraud, who was a former employee of the Southern Pacific Railroad. It was located across the street from the railroad depot. Giraud was an Alpine Frenchman who in 1902 married Marie Jeanne Moynier, whose father was from the Upper Alps and her mother from the Lower Pyrenees. After the Commercial Hotel was destroyed by fire in 1912, Giraud invested the insurance money in sheep. Before driving them to

Tehachapi: Little Béarn

summer pasture he erected a tent on the hotel site, leaving a temporarily housed saloon in charge of another Frenchman. Upon returning he found that his associate had absconded with everything. Giraud was killed in a tractor accident in 1929, and his widow married Jean Zampa, a native of the Upper Alps, who was one of several part owners of the Imperial Hotel in East Bakersfield. As the years went by many of the Tehachapi Valley French moved elsewhere, including several families which went to East Bakersfield in order to be nearer the heart of the French colony of Kern County.

The Giraud family. Clockwise: Jennie (Moynier) Giraud, Eugene, Martha, Herc (Cyrille), Cyrille Sr., and Harry. (Photo courtesy of Harry Giraud)

A Laffargue family portrait. Back row: Marie, Josephine, Pete, Eddie. Front row: Pierre, Anna, Henry, Madeleine. (Photo courtesy of Anna Laffargue Coe)

Jean Baptiste Capdeville and his wife, the former Anna Fillet. (Photo courtesy of Marcelle Reynaud Borel)

François "Frank" Bernard with his wife Marie and brother-in-law Joe Pellisson. (Photo courtesy of Marcelle Reynaud Borel)

Tehachapi in 1903. Note in upper left of picture the old schoolhouse (with belfry) which became the Tehachapi Hotel. (Photo courtesy of Felix Etcheverry)

The French Hotel (far left of picture) of Tehachapi in 1889. (Photo courtesy of Herb and Ola Mae Force)

Playing Pedro at the Tehachapi Hotel. Left to right: Jacques Oddous, Arnoux Faure (seated), two unknowns, Joe Pellisson, Jean Zampa, and Pete Raymond.

The Commercial Hotel. (Photo courtesy of Anna Laffargue Coe)

The Franco-American Hotel, previously the Basko, with handball court in 1916. (Photo courtesy of Herb and Ola Mae Force)

The Tehachapi Hotel on the southwest corner of F and Green Streets in 1916. (Photo courtesy of Herb and Ola Mae Force)

CHAPTER X

The French In The Oil Era

In the mid-1860s, simultaneously with the rise of mining activity around Havilah in the Sierra Nevada, the commercial exploitation of petroleum deposits began in the San Joaquin Valley. Until then the pioneers had made only limited use of the crude petroleum that oozed from "tar springs," including the marking of sheep and the lubricating of noisy wagon wheel bearings. When the commercial development of the petroleum deposits began in the 1860s, it was under the mining laws adopted in the state in the early 1850s.

Interest in the development of the petroleum deposits found north of Buena Vista Lake was developing when Stephen Bond, a Mariposa miner, went on a prospecting trip to the region in the summer of 1863. Early in 1864 a group of Mariposa County businessmen, among them James M. Ketton and Talleyrand Choisier, formed the Buena Vista Petroleum Company. The latter's French name obscures his Illinois origins, from whence he had come during the gold rush. Among their Mariposa County neighbors were several other businessmen who later became prominent in Kern County, including Beneditto Ardizzi, Louis V. Olcese, and James De Pauli.

Upon the organization of the Buena Vista Petroleum Company, the founders enlisted the help of Mon. E. Benoist, a San Francisco chemist. His optimistic report on the quality of the crude petroleum was available in the spring of 1864, and this was one of the earliest, if not the first, geographical reports on the petroleum resources of the San Joaquin Valley. From it, he reported, could be derived illuminating and lubricating oils, as well as products that could be used as fuel or converted to gas.

Lest We Forget

In the spring of 1865 the San Francisco *Alta California* reported that Benoist had demonstrated that kerosene made from the Buena Vista petroleum burned just as brilliantly as did that from Pennsylvania. Although the petroleum under development north of Buena Vista Lake could be refined into acceptable illuminating and lubricating oils, the marketing of these products had to await the development of better transportation before they could be profitably marketed.

Many of the French sheepmen of Kern County at one time or another owned oil-bearing land with the all-important mineral rights, but few of them actually "struck it rich" during the oil boom which started late in the 1890s. Yet many of the leases carried the names of the luckless original owners. The Lambert leases are excellent examples.

Peter Lambert's career encompassed gold mining, sheep raising, and oil development in Kern County. A native of the Upper Alps, he was a young man when he joined his uncle Jean Roux in far away Los Angeles, California. Lambert made at least two treks up and down the state as a herder in the employ of his uncle. While doing so he was confronted by cattlemen who tied and dragged him behind a horse, an experience that caused him to walk with a slight limp for the rest of his life. By the mid-1870s he and his newly-arrived brothers had flocks of their own in the Delano area. The devastating drought of the late 1870s convinced Lambert of the importance of owning one's own land, and he acquired well over one thousand acres of range land. In mid-1883 he married Malvina Rambaud, a native of the Upper Alps, and they became residents of East Bakersfield. Lambert sold seven sections of land to Henry Miller, a well-known cattleman, and then subsequently when petroleum was discovered on the property during the oil boom he tried to have the sale declared null and void because his wife had not signed the papers. His claim had no validity, however, since it was pointed out that he had acquired the land before his marriage.

In contrast to the meager beginnings of the oil industry in Kern County with the formation of the Buena Vista Petroleum Company in the mid-1860s, oil developments were in full swing

The French In The Oil Era

by the opening of the twentieth century. Although French interest in oil was apparent, it was not on the scale of the French interest in the earlier gold mining and sheep raising activities. Among the French businessmen active in the oil towns was Jean Casenave, a native of the Lower Pyrenees, proprietor of the Pioneer Bakery at Fellows, and who took as a partner compatriot Thomas Lacoste. Among their employees was Pierre Jean Aubin, a native of the Upper Alps, who, after finding neither New York nor New Orleans to his liking, had come to Kern County. In later years he became the county's most peripatetic baker, never working long at any shop, working at different times at the Parisian and Golden Crust in Bakersfield, and the French in East Bakersfield. Even after retirement in 1937 he found the lure of dough so strong that he occasionally wandered to a place of former employment until his wife or children came looking for him.

Another of Kern County's French businessmen who settled in the oil towns was Baptiste Bergès, whose older brothers Alexander and Jean B. Bergès lived in the Bakersfield area. A native of the Lower Pyrenees, Bap, as he was familiarly known, turned from sheep raising to saloon keeping in the Sunset District. He married Anna Cazassus, also a native of the Lower Pyrenees, at the Hotel Estalia in Bishop, whose untimely death in 1913 occurred during the birth of triplets, only one of whom, a boy, lived. The baby and his elder brother were raised by Bergès, while a daughter was cared for by her uncle, Auguste Cazassus, and his wife, who were proprietors of the French Laundry at Bishop.

Among Kern County's petroleum-related businesses was the Franco-Western Oil Company. In 1918 the firm's co-founders, Edmond Chopy and his brother-in-law Henri Gaillochet, invested in oil properties in Wyoming and Texas. Initially the company was known as the Franco-Wyoming, but after subsidiaries were added, including the MacElroy Ranch Company in Texas, the Franco-Central in Kansas, and in the late 1920s properties near McKittrick of the Franco-Western in California, the name of the firm was changed to Franco-Western Oil Company. Louis

Gaillochet, the son of Henri Gaillochet, was named president of Franco-Wyoming, and Harry Campbell was selected for the same position with Franco-Western. In the mid-1950s the various branches of the firm were consolidated under the corporate name of Franco-Western Oil Company, and in 1961 the firm's offices were established at Bakersfield. In 1965 the Franco-Western holdings were sold to the Mobil Oil Corporation.

Another of Kern County's French-owned oil firms was founded at a time when the national economy was depressed in the mid-1930s. Conrad Schlumberger, a native of Alsace, formed the Schlumberger Well Surveying Corporation. Its Bakersfield office was managed by Jacques Gallois, a charter member of the Bakersfield Petroleum Club and a highly respected resident of the community.

In the meantime young Frenchmen had spent their vacations working in the Kern County oil fields and a few of them determined to become permanent residents of the United States.

James De Pauli, one of the many Italians with French connections. (Photo courtesy of Thelma De Pauli Campbell)

Pierre "Pete" Lambert, pioneer sheepman in Kern County and one of many Frenchmen to lose out on the oil boom.

The 1907 wedding photo of Joseph Bresson and Mary Roux. Standing: Ernest Bresson, Pierre "Pete" Lambert and his daughter Marie. Seated: Agnes Plantier, Joseph Bresson, and his bride Mary Roux. (Photo courtesy of Helen Chevalier Johnson)

Lest We Forget

The Pioneer Bakery in Fellows, circa 1909, with Thomas Lacoste, owner Jean Casenave, and Pierre Jean "Pete" Aubin. (Photo courtesy of Jeanne Abadie Edmondson)

"Bap" Bergès, youngest of the four Bergès brothers. (Photo courtesy of Bertha Bergès Gates)

The Franco-Western oil field near McKittrick. (Photo courtesy of J. Guy)

The French In The Oil Era

The Franco-Western office at 3132 18th Street. (Photo courtesy of J. Guy)

Louis Gaillochet, president of Franco-Wyoming, with Harry Duncan Campbell, head of Franco-Western. (Photo courtesy of J. Guy)

Jacques Gallois, head of the Bakersfield office of the Schlumberger Company. (Photo courtesy of the Petroleum Club of Bakersfield)

California State College, Bakersfield, with sheep grazing in the foreground.

EPILOGUE

In May 1974, growing out of a project undertaken by the first group of graduating French majors at California State College, Bakersfield, a banquet was held at the Maison Jaussaud restaurant for those descendants of the original colony and recent French immigrants interested in keeping alive the French heritage and traditions in Kern County. As a result of that dinner meeting, there exists today Le Club Français de Bakersfield dedicated to the promotion of French culture.

On September 1, 1976, a Bicentennial ceremony was held in International Square located in East Bakersfield at the intersection of Sumner and Baker Streets. A plaque dedicated to the founding of Sumner in October 1874 was unveiled by the Kern County Historical Society and the Kern County Museum.

The park itself was the result of a proposal made in 1970 to the City Council by former councilman Walter F. Heisey. An agreement was finally reached with the Southern Pacific Railroad Company by which the City rented the site for the amount of the property tax involved. Today the area surrounding the Square is known as International Village and the United States and California flags wave an aerial salute not only to the French but to the brave pioneers of many nations who settled in Sumner beginning over a century ago.

APPENDIX

SELECTED FRENCH PLACE NAMES IN AND AROUND KERN COUNTY

Beau Canyon—a descriptive name meaning beautiful canyon, it is located in the Tehachapi Mountains south of the Tehachapi Valley.

Bernard Street (Bakersfield)—named for James A. Bernard, the son of Arsène P. Bernard. It forms the northern boundary of the Bernard Addition in East Bakersfield.

Borel Powerhouse—located near the upper end of Kern River Canyon, it was named for Antoine Borel, an early partner of Henry E. Huntington and William G. Kerchoff, founders of the Kern Power Company, a subsidiary of Pacific Light and Power Company.

Borel Street (Delano)—named for Auguste Borel, who was an early French sheepman-turned-hotelkeeper.

Chanac Creek—flowing west out of the Tehachapi Mountains, it was named for François Channac, an early French settler in Cummings Valley.

Chevalier Road (Greenfield)—named for Emile Chevalier, a French sheepman who turned to farming and settled in the area.

Eugene Grade (Greenhorn Mountains)—named for Eugène Caillaud, a French gold miner who settled in these mountains in 1859 and operated a store on Greenhorn Creek.

Franco-Western Road—located east of Reward, it was named for the Franco-Western Oil Company, which today is a part of Mobil Oil.

French Gulch—located west of Lake Isabella, it was named for an incident involving some Frenchmen who jumped the claim of a miner named Walker. Walker reportedly killed them.

Appendix

French Meadow—located in the Sierra Nevada on Kelso Creek, it probably was a favorite grazing site for the flocks of French sheepherders.

Girard Street (Delano)—named in honor of the Girard brothers, Joseph, Jules, and Philippe, who were French ranchers.

Grimaud Creek—located north of Bakersfield, it probably was named for Stanislaus Grimaud, a French sheepman.

Lebec—located thirty-six miles south of Bakersfield, this town was named for Peter Lebeck, thought to be a French Canadian fur trapper killed by a bear at the future site of Fort Tejon in 1837.

Loraine—a town in Caliente Canyon established by two French miners. Originally known as Paris, the name was changed to Loraine, after the French province of Lorraine, to distinguish the community from Perris in Riverside County.

Loustalot Lane (Bakersfield)—named by the Bakersfield City Council as a tribute to John Loustalot, former Kern County Sheriff and late Bakersfield Postmaster. He was the son of a pioneer Béarnais couple, Pierre and Félicie (Labrucherie) Loustalot.

Nadeau Street (California City)—named for Rémi Nadeau, a French Canadian teamster who hauled bullion between Owens Valley and Los Angeles.

Napoleon Spring—located in the Temblor Range in western Kern County, it was named for Napoléon Bonaparte (1769-1821), emperor of France.

Pellisier Road (Cummings Valley)—named for François Pellissier, who was a French homesteader in the area.

Sirretta Peak (Tulare County)—located north of the Kern County line in the Sierra Nevada, it was named for Hippolyte Sarret, a French sheepman who settled in Poso Flat. There is also a Siretta Street in Kernville.

BIBLIOGRAPHY

BOOKS

Bailey, Richard C. *Kern County Place Names.* Bakersfield, California: Kern County Historical Society. 1967.

Barès, Florence and Marcel. *Le Western Champsaurin.* Gap, France: Editions Ophrys. 1976.

Barras, Judy. *The Long Road to Tehachapi.* Tehachapi, California: Private printing. 1976.

Boyd, William Harland. *A California Middle Border.* Richardson, Texas: The Havilah Press. 1972.

Caughey, John Walton. *The California Gold Rush.* Los Angeles: The University of California Press. 1948.

Guinn, J. M. *History of the State of California and Biographical Record of the San Joaquin Valley, California.* Chicago: The Chapman Publishing Company. 1905.

Hansen, Marcus Lee. *The Immigrant in American History.* New York: Harper and Row. 1940.

Hill, Laurance L. *La Reina—Los Angeles in Three Centuries.* Los Angeles: The Security First National Bank. 1929.

Histoire de la Ville de Gap. Publiée sous les auspices de la Société d'Etudes des Hautes Alpes, n.d.

History of Kern County, California, with Illustrations. San Francisco: Wallace Elliot and Company. 1883.

Latta, F. F. *Black Gold in the Joaquin.* Caldwell, Idaho: Caxton Printers, Ltd. 1949.

Lévy, Daniel. *Les Français en Californie.* San Francisco: Grégoire, Tauzy et Cie. 1884.

Miller, Thelma B. *History of Kern County, California.* Chicago: The S. J. Clarke Publishing Company. 1929.

Bibliography

Morgan, Wallace M. *A History of Kern County, California.* Los Angeles: Historic Record Company. 1914.

Nasatir, Abraham P. *French Activities in California.* Palo Alto, California: Stanford University Press. 1945.

Nasatir, A. P. *A French Journalist in the California Gold Rush - The Letters of Etienne Derbec.* Georgetown, California: The Talisman Press. 1964.

Newmark, Harris. *Sixty Years in Southern California.* New York: Houghton-Mifflin. 1930.

Soule, Frank, John H. Gihon and James Nisbet. *The Annals of San Francisco.* New York: D. Appleton and Company. 1854.

Stephenson, George M. *A History of American Immigration 1820-1924.* New York: Ginn and Company. 1926.

Vandor, Paul E. *History of Fresno County.* Los Angeles: Historic Record Company. 1919.

Where the Railroad Ended. A History of Delano, 1873-1973. Delano, California: Delano Centennial Board. 1974.

BULLETINS

Historic Kern, Quarterly Bulletin of the Kern County Historical Society, Vol. 7, No. 4, June 1957.

The Plow, Publication of the Delano Historical Society, Vols. 3 - 10, 1969-1974.

NEWSPAPERS

Alta California. San Francisco, California. February 1855 - June 1859.

Bakersfield Californian. Bakersfield, California. February 1897 - December 1899.

Daily Californian. Bakersfield, California. April 1891 - February 1897.

Delano Record. Delano, California. September 29, 1908 - December 31, 1920.

Havilah Miner. Havilah, California. June 1872 - May 1874.

Lest We Forget

Havilah Weekly Courier. Havilah, California. October 1866 - December 1869.

Holograph. Delano, California. May 29, 1908-August 1, 1908.

Kern County Californian. Bakersfield, California. December 1879 - March 1891.

Kern County Weekly Courier. Bakersfield, California. December 1869 - May 1876.

Kern County Weekly Gazette. Bakersfield, California. 1876 - 1885.

Morning Echo. Kern City, California. 1902 - 1903.

Southern Californian. Bakersfield, California. May 1875 - December 1879.

INDEX

Abadie, Alexandre, 104, *133*
Abadie, Marceline Lacoste, 104, *117, 133*
Abonel, Léon, *14*, 19, 101, 120
Abonel, Lydie Bécaïs, 19, *120*
Adobe Station, 28
Alexis, Frank, *52*
Alley Bank, 98
Alps Hotel (Bakersfield), 60
Alps Mountains, 15, 16, 17, 18, 19, 23
Amar, Auguste, 62
Amour, Augustin, 102, *124, 125*
Amourig Stables, *14*
amusements, 20, 22, 48, 52, 53-54, 58, 101, 104
Amy, Claude Benoît, 95-96, *106*
Amy, Victoire Julie Deboissy, 96, *106*
Amy, Victor Louis, 95-97, *107*
Amy and Ardizzi Store, 97, *105, 107*
Ancelle, 7, 15, 16, 28, 76, 100, 101
André, André, 18, 28, 30
André, Cyrille, 28, *36*
André, Marie Barthélemy, 28
Ardizzi, Beneditto, 47, 96-98, *107*, 143
Ardizzi-Olcese Company, 47, 48, 97-98, *105*, 238
Ariey, Auguste, 62
Asher, Jacob, 54, 58
Aubin, Pierre Jean, 77, *125*, 145, *148*

Baillif, Julien Alexandre, 5
Baker, Thomas, 57
bakers, 54, 62, 77, 100, 101-102, 145
Bakersfield, 20, 29, 30, 48, 54, 57-70, 95, 104, 145, 146
Bakersfield Seed and Feed Store, 62
bankers, 47, 59, 74, 75, 97, 98, *108*
bankruptcy, 47, 48, 59, 73, 79, 98
barbers, 62
Bareille, Simon, 28
Barthélemy, Jean, 103, *128*
Barthélemy, Léa Bonhomme Isnard, *10*, 103, *128*
Basko Hotel (Tehachapi), 136, 141
Basques, xi, xiii, 18, 19, 22, 60, 61, 62, 101, 102, 103, 135, 136
Bastille Day, *12*, 20, 21, 22, *52*, 97
Bayes, Jacques, *126*
Béarn Province, 7, 15
Beaudry, Edward, 4

Bécas, Louis, 30, *52*
Bello, Ramona, 26-27, *35*
Benoist, E., 143-144
Bergès, Alexander, 28, 60, *69*, 145
Bergès, Anna Cazassus, 145
Bergès, Baptiste, *69*, 145, *148*
Bergès, Jean Baptiste, 60-61, *69, 70, 113*, 145
Bergès, Jean Pierre, *69*
Bergès, Margaret Roquette, 28
Bergès, Marie Inda, 60, *70*
Bernamayou, Pierre, 27, 47
Bernard, Arsène Peter, 98-99, *109*, 152
Bernard, Blanche Sarret, 26, *33*
Bernard, Clophine, 99, *110*
Bernard, Corrennah, *110*
Bernard, Edith "Maggie" Long, 99, *110*
Bernard, Elzira, 98, 99, *109*
Bernard, François, 136, *139*
Bernard, James A. (Jr.), *110*
Bernard, James A. (Sr.), 99, *110*, 152
Bernard, Marie Pellisson, 136, *139*
Bernard, Virgile, 5, 26, *33*
Bertrand, Anaïs Aubin, 77
Bertrand, Joseph, 77, *93*
Bidibas, Augustin, 45-46
Billiard Saloon (Havilah), 54-55
Bimat, Bernard, 7, 18
Bimat, Edward, 7
Bimat, Léon, 7, 18
Bimat, Malvina Rostain, 7, 18
Bimat, Marie Rostain, 7, 18
Bishop, 48, *51*, 102, *126*, 145
Bizac, Jean Pierre, 4
blacksmiths, 103, *111, 127*
Blanc, Eli, 103, *112, 130*
Blanc, Louise Raymond, 103, *130*
Boisseau, Jean, 3
Boisseranc, Louise Bernard-Raymond, *118*
Boisseranc, Marie Richaud, *43*
Boisseranc, Zéphirin, *117, 118*
Borel, Alice, *12*, 21
Borel, Antoine, 152
Borel, Auguste, 76, *86, 87*, 152
Borel, Félicie Espitallier, 48, *50*
Borel, Julie Rambaud, 101, *118*
Borel, Justin, 101, *118*
Borel, Louis, *51*

Borel, Madeleine, *112, 115*
Borel, Marie Labarthe, 76, *86, 87*
Borel, Romulus Petrus, 48, *50, 112, 122*
Borgas, Serre, 3
Bouelle, Auguste, 5
Bresson, Ernest (Jr.), *51*
Bresson, Ernest (Sr.), *51, 147*
Bresson, Joseph, *51, 52*, 102, *115, 147*
Bresson, Marie Roux, *147*
Bresson, Suzie, *51*
Bresson, Victor, 135
Brignaudy, Marie Thérèse, 62
Brown House (Delano), 74, *79*
Buena Vista Petroleum Company, 143, 144
Burgemaster, Louise Richaud, *118*
businessmen, 3, 26, 28, 47, 48, 53, 54, 57-62, *63-65, 67-68*, 71-78, *79, 83*, 95-103, *105-108, 111-112, 114, 115, 117-127*, 135-137, *140-142*, 145-146

Caillaud, Charles, 25, *32*, 60
Caillaud, Eugène, 3, 25, 152
Caillaud, Frances Guillon, 25, *32*
Caliente, 2, 5, 58
California Bakery (East Bakersfield), 102, *125*
California State College, Bakersfield, *150*, 151
Campbell, Harry, 146, *149*
Capdeville, Anna Fillet, 136, *138*
Capdeville, Jean Baptiste, 136, *138*
Casenave, Jean, 145, *148*
Castagnet, Albert, 77
cattlemen, 25, 26, 27, *32, 35*, 74
Cazassus, Anna, 102, *125, 126*, 145
Cazassus, Auguste, 102, *125, 126*, 145
Cerro Gordo Freighting Company, 5
Cesmat, Eliza Roquette, 100
Cesmat, Frances Mouliot, *35*, 100, *113*
Cesmat, Jean, 100
Cesmat, Joseph, 78-79, *94*
Cesmat, Juliette Escallier, 79
Cesmat, Marius, 100, *111, 112, 113, 114*, 136
Cesmat Hotel (East Bakersfield), 100, *114*
Chabraie, Etienne, 5
Chabre, Pete, *121*
Chabre, Virginia Blanc, *128*
Champsaur Valley, 7, 15, 74
Channac, François, 26-27, *35*, 47, 152
Chastan, Octave, *37*
Chauvet, Louis, *52*
Chauvin, Emile, 71-72, 73, 74
Chevalier, Emile, *121*, 152
Chevalier, Jean B., 2

Chevalier, Justin, *9*, 18
Chevalier, Marie Etchebarne, *9*, 18
Choisier, Talleyrand, 143
Chopy, Edmond, 145
churches, 18, 22, *91*, 104
Civil War, 25, 53
Clerou family, *9*
Club Français de Bakersfield, Le, 151
Commercial Hotel (Bakersfield), 60
Commercial Hotel (Tehachapi), 136, *141*
cooks, 54, 57-58
Cordier, Léon, 62
corrals (sheep), 26, 28, 72, 74, 95
Couvreur, Jean B., 3
crimes, 5, 45-46, 72, 137
Cummings Valley, 26, 27, *35*, 47, 152, 153

dairymen, 27
Dauphiné Province, 7, 15, 16
Davin, Joseph, 30
Davin, Pierre, 30
de la Borde, Claude, 2, 3, 4, 53
De Pauli, James, 143, *146*
de St. Jean, Félix S., 4
de Yough, Madame, 62
Delagne, Jules, *12, 52*
Delano, 28, 71-78, *79, 87, 91, 92*, 144, 152, 153
Delano Hardware Store, 75
Delano Hotel, 76, *86*
depressions, 26, 47, 48, 59, 71, 75, 79, 98, 146
Doriot, Charles Henri, 4
Drago, Théophile, 3
Drake, Frank, 5
droughts, 28, 45-46, 47
Druids, 29, 104
du Rau, Adrien Defos, 72-73
Ducommun, Armand, 62
Dufour, Frank, 136
Duquesne, Félix Désiré, 96, *107*
Duquesne, Mathilde Amy, 96, *106*
Dusserre, Auguste, 75, *85*
Dusserre, Jacques, 20, 101
Dusserre, Paulin, 75, *85*

East Bakersfield, xii, xiii, 18, 19, 20, 22, 23, 28, 47, 61, 73, 95-133, 137, 152
entertainment. *See* amusements.
Escaiche, François, 54
Escalet, Ernest, 57-58
Escallier, André, *51*
Escallier, Antoine, 76, *87*
Escallier, Cécile Le Flohic, 29-30, *42*
Escallier, Ida Moreau, 77, 79, *90*
Escallier, Jean Pierre, 17
Escallier, Joseph, 29

Index

Escallier, Jules, 76-77, 79, *90*
Escallier, Léon, 76-77, *87, 88*
Espitallier, Anaïs Philipp, 100, *116*
Espitallier, Appolonie Eyraud, 102, *122*
Espitallier, Etienne, *49, 51*
Espitallier, François "Frank," *49*, 100, *116*
Espitallier, Frank, 46
Espitallier, "Gros" Jean, *49, 52, 123*
Espitallier, Henri, *12, 52, 123*
Espitallier, Jean "Sprit," *51*
Espitallier, Joseph, *8, 10, 50, 52*, 102, 123
Espitallier, Léa Grimaud, *8*
Espitallier, Lucille Pellisson, *11, 114*
Espitallier, Marius, *111*
Espitallier, Marius Martin, 101-102, *112, 122*, 123
Esponda, George, 136
Estribou, Jean B., 99, 103, *111*
Estribou, Sophie Laborde, 103, *130*
Eugene Grade, 3
Eustache, Anaïs Escallier, *86*
Eyraud, Auguste Pierre, 25, 59-60, *61, 67, 68, 70*, 112
Eyraud, Augustine Bertrand, 29, *38*
Eyraud, Constance Marin, 101
Eyraud, Eli, *12*, 17
Eyraud, Emily Prayer, 29, *40*
Eyraud, Eugène, 16
Eyraud, François, *37*
Eyraud, Jean, 17, 20, 101, *112, 121*
Eyraud, Joseph, 29, *39*
Eyraud, "Long Valley" Joe, 17, 28-29, *37, 38*
Eyraud, Marie Louise Allemand, *114*
Eyraud, Rosalie Caillaud, 60, *68, 70*

family life, xiii, 18, 19, 22, 23, 76, 79, 104
Famoso, 77, 78-79, *93*
farmers, xiii, 4, 28, 29, 30, *44*, 48, 74, 78, 99, 104
Farran, John, 4
Faure, Alphonse, 20
Faure, Arnoux, *141*
Faure, Cyril, 74-75
Faure, Dominic, 46
Faure, Joseph, 67, 74-75
Faure, Louise Borel Escallier, 77, *86, 88, 89*
Faure, Pierre, 74-75, 77, *89*
Faure, Pierre "de l'ours," *112*
Faure Brothers' Store (Delano), 75, *83*
Feather River, xii, 1, 29, *37*
fires, 59, 60, 72, 100-102, *114*, 135, 136
foreign miners' tax, 1-2
Franco-American Hotel (Tehachapi) *See* Basko Hotel.

Franco-Prussian War, 15, 96
Franco-Western Oil Company, 145-146, 148, *149*, 152
freighters, 5, 71
French Bakery (East Bakersfield), 102, *123, 125*, 145
French Camp, xii
French Canadians, xii, 1, 4, 5, 27, 59, 103, 153
French Gulch, 152
French Hospital (San Francisco), 97, 99, *110*
French Hotel (19th St. and Chester Ave., Bakersfield), 57-58, *64*
French Hotel (19th St. and M St., Bakersfield), 60, *67*
French Hotel (Delano), 72
French Hotel (Sumner), 99
French Hotel (Tehachapi), 135, *140*
French House (Cesmat, East Bakersfield), 100, *111*
French House (Plantier, East Bakersfield), *9, 52*, 100, 101, *112, 114, 115*
French Laundry (Bishop), 102-103, *126*, 145
French Liquor Store (Bakersfield), 60
French Meadow, 153
French Ranch, 25, *32*, 60
French Restaurant (Bakersfield), 57
French Restaurant (Sumner), 99
fur trappers, xi-xii, 27, 153

Gaillochet, Henri, 145-146
Gaillochet, Louis, 145-146, *149*
Galland, Alexina Viau, *124*
Galland, Elysée, *52, 124*
Galland, Jean, 102, *124*
Galland's Bakery (East Bakersfield), 102
Gallien, Joseph, 100
Gallois, Jacques, 146, *149*
Galtes, Pablo, 60, *70*
Gap Hotel (East Bakersfield), 100
Garnier, Jules, *120*
Gil, Marie Prayer, *40*
Girard, Anaïs Brochier, 76
Girard, Eva Chabot, 76
Girard, Joseph, 76, 153
Girard, Jules, 76, 153
Girard, Philippe, 76, 153
Girard, Thérèse Marie Motte, 76
Giraud, Cyrille, 136-137, *137*
Giraud, Jennie Moynier. *See* Zampa.
Godey, Alexis, 27, *59*
gold rushes, 1, 2, 3, 16, 71, 96, 143
Golden Gate Hotel (Havilah), 53-54, 55
Gouglat, Auguste, *4*, 53
Granite Station, 26, 101

Lest We Forget

Greenhorn Mountains, 3, 5, 25, 60
Grimaud, Stanislaus, 153
Gueydan, Joseph, 102, *124*
Gueydan, Léa Marin, 102

Harpending, Asbury, 3, 53
Havilah, 4, 53-55, 57, 58, 143
holidays, *12*, 20-21, 22, *52*
Hollis, Marie. *See* Marie Le Flohic.
Hôtel des Alpes (East Bakersfield), 102
hotelkeepers, 22, 26, 53, 54, 55, 57, 58, 59-60, *67*, 72, 73, 76-77, 78, 96, 99-101, 135-137, 152
Hourdé, Constant, 5
Hudson Bay Company, xii

Imperial Hotel (East Bakersfield), 101
Iribarne, John, 135
Isnard, Théophile, 103, *127, 128*
Italians, xiii, 19, 22, 48, 61-62, 104, 146

Jaussaud, Dermide (Babe), *119*
Jaussaud, Emile, *120*
Jaussaud, Ermance (Garnier), *119*
Jaussaud, Martin (Jr.), *119, 120*
Jaussaud, Martin (Sr.), 101, *119, 120*
journalism, 19, 20, 54, 55

Kern City. *See* East Bakersfield.
Kern City French Bakery. *See* French Bakery.
Kern River, xii, 2, 3, 25, 57
Kernville, 2, 3, 5, 58
Keskydees, 1
Ketton, James M., 143
Keyesville, 3, 53

Laborde, Pierre "Pete," *124*
Lacoste, Thomas, 145, *148*
Laffargue, Madeleine Fillet, 136, *138*
Laffargue, Pierre, 136, *138*
Lafont, Marie Achin, *133*
Lafont, Valentin, *133*
Lafontaine, Edouard, 99-100
Laframboise, Michel, xi
Lagier, Auguste, 17, 77-78
Lagier, Jean Pierre, 29
Lambert, Malvina Rambaud, 28, 144
Lambert, Marie, *147*
Lambert, Peter, 28, *112,* 144, *147*
Laxague, Pierre, 102, *123*
Le Flohic, Lucien, 30
Le Flohic, Mabel Hollis, 30
Le Flohic, Marie, 30, *42*
Lebec, 153
Lebec, Pierre (Peter Lebeck), xii, 153
Legrain, Charles, 3

Lestelle, Pierre, 4
Lorrette, Emile, 3
Los Angeles, xi, 5, 16, 18, 27, 48, 58, 144, 153
Louis, Charles B., 2
Loustalot, John, 153

Maison Dorée, La, 58
Mandis, Frances Saiz, 73-74, *79*
Mandis, Jean Adrien, 72-74, *80*
Martin, Anastasie Escallier, *34*
Martin, Auguste, *14, 34*
Martin, Martin, 5, 18, *34*
Martinto, John B., 62
Matheron, Alphonsine Marin, 104, *132*
Matheron, Elie J., *13*, 16, 104, *132*
Maurel, Auguste, *112, 119*
Metropole Meat Market (East Bakersfield), 99, *111*
Michel, Auguste M., 62
Michel, Eloi, *12*
military service, 16, 21, 22-23
miners, xii, 1-6, 25-26, 53, 57, 71, 73, 96, 103, 143, 152, 153
Mon, Catherine Cazaux, 26, *34*
Mon, Vincent, 26, *34*
Mon Creek, Canyon, and Bluff, 26
Morel, Julien, 78
Mouliot, Laura, *35, 113*
Mouliot, Martin, 27, *35*
Mouliot, Refugia Bello, 26-27, *35*

Nadeau, Rémi, 5, 153
National Hotel (East Bakersfield), 101, *117*, 118
naturalization, 2, 4-5
New Central Hotel (Delano), 77
New Commercial Hotel (East Bakersfield), 101
New Commercial Saloon (East Bakersfield), *121*
Nicolas, Maurice, 30
Noriega, Faustino, 61, *70, 112*
Noriega, Louise Inda, 61, *70*

Oddous, Jean Baptiste, 30, *120, 132*
Oddous, Emile, *120*
Oddous, Jacques, 30, *44, 141*
oil boom, xiii, 28, 62, 95, 143-150
oilmen, 60, 143-146
Olcese, Louis Virgin, 47, 97-98, *107, 108*, 143
Ollivier, Désiré, 30
Ollivier, Victorine Nicolas, 30
Oloron Ste. Marie, *9*, 15, 27, 28, 60
Orcier, Léon, *126*
Orcier, Marie Mélanie Morel, 78, *94*

Index

Orcier, Romulus, 78, *94*
Oriot, Edward, 5

Pacific Improvement Company, 78
Paquette, Prosper, 103, *111*, 127
parades, *12*, 21, *52*
Parisian Bakery (Bakersfield), 62, 102
Pellissier, François, 27, 153
Pellissier, Germain, 27
Pellissier, Jeanne Seinturier, 27
Pellissier, Nicolas, 27
Pellisson, Joseph, 136, *138, 141*
Perrier, Angéline, 75, *84*
Perrier, Auguste, 75, *84*
Perrier, Joseph, 75, *85*
Perriers' Saloon (Delano), 75, *84*
Petersburg, 3
Philipp, Auguste, *51*
Philipp, Jean, 61, 101, 116, *119*
Philipp, Jeannette, 51, *120*
Philipp, Marcelle, *8, 10*
Philipp, Marie Louise, *120*
Philippe, Frank, *112*
Philippe, Philippe, 18
Pioneer Bakery (Fellows), 145, *148*
Pioneer Hotel (Famoso), 78, *93*
place names (French), xii, 3, 25, 26, 27, *31, 32,* 71, 99, 152-153
Plantier, Agnes, *114, 147*
Plantier, Marie Espitallier, 100, *114, 115*
Plantier, Marius, *9*, 100, *112, 114, 115*
politics, 1-2, 15, 53, 54, 97, 98-99
Ponsard, Victor, 4
Poso Flat, 25, 26, *33*
Pourroy, Emilie Villard, 104
Pourroy, Jean, 104
Prel, Jean, 27
Prel, Noémi Moncoronel, 27
prohibition, 22, 75, 78
Provensal, Félicie Bonhomme, 103, *129*
Provensal, Fidèle, *49*
Provensal, François, 103, *129*
Pyrenees Bakery (East Bakersfield), 102, 123
Pyrenees Mountains, 15, 16, 18, 19, 22, 23, 48

Rag Gulch, 74, *82*
railroads. *See* Southern Pacific Railroad and Vaca Valley Railroad.
Rambaud, Pete, *127*
Rambaud, Rose Raymond, 103
Rambaud, Vincent, 103, 127
Rantz,, Jacob, 54
Raymond, Jean A. (Jr.), *51, 131*
Raymond, Jean A. (Sr.), *51*, 103, *131*
Raymond, Jean B., 103-104, *112*, 131
Raymond, Marie Cazanave, *11, 51*
Raymond, Marie Galvin, 103, *130*
Raymond, Pierre "Peter," 29, *51*, 101, 103, *141*
Raymond, Rose Eyraud, *51*, 103, *131*
Relixto, Barin, 20
restaurateurs, 26, 53, 57-58, 72, 99, 101, *120*, 135, 151
Reynaud, Hortense, *92*
Reynaud, Marcel, 77, *92*, 102
Reynier, Armand, *51*
Richaud, Lucienne Le Flohic, 29, *42*
Richaud, Simon, 29, *41*
Robert, Jean, 5
Robert, Robert, 18
Roquette, Dora Cervantes, 28
Roquette, Peter Prosper, 28
Rostain, Célestin, 75
Rostain, Fidèle, *49, 52*
Roux, Ernest, 61, *63*
Roux, Jean, 144
Roux, Louis, *51*, 61, *63*
Roux, Louise Philipp, 61, *63, 66, 120*
Roux, Marie, *12*, 21, *51, 63, 120*
Roux, Marius, *51*
Roux, Octave, 61, *63, 56*
Roux Grocery Store, 61, *63*
Rufener, Marie Louise Nougier, *114*

St. Joseph's Catholic Church (East Bakersfield), 18, 22
St. Mary's Catholic Church (Delano), *91*
St. Regis Hotel (Bakersfield), 60
saloonkeepers, 26, 60, *57, 68*, 75, 78, *84*, 101, 102, 137, 145
San Francisco, xi, 16, 18, *34*, 53, 55, 61, 96, 97, 101
San Joaquin Valley, xi, xii, 17, 23, 25, 28-30, 45, 71, 143
Sarret, Hippolyte, 25-26, *31*, 153
Sarret, Juliette Caillaud, 25, *33*
Sartiat, Bernard, 27, *43*, 101
Sartiat, Bernard Pierre, *43, 118*
Sartiat, Marie Louise Richaud, *43, 117*
Sartiat, Pierre, 27, *43*, 101, *117, 118*
Saulque, Frank, *51*
Schlumberger, Conrac, 146
Schlumberger Well Surveying Corporation, 146, *149*
Seinturier, Jean, *119*
Seinturier, Mary, *92*
Seinturier, Victor, *92*
Selna, Silvio, *128*
sheep trails, 45-52
sheepmen, xii, xiii, 25, 26, 27, 28, 29, 30, *31, 37*, 45-48, *49-51*, 61, 72, 74, 75, 76, 77, 78, 79, 97, 98, 100, 101, 103, 104, *127*, 136-137, 144, 145, *147*, 152, 153

Lest We Forget

shoemakers, 2, 77, *93*
Sierra Nevada, 2, 4, 5, 25, *31*, 45, 153
Sirretta Peak, 25, 31, 153
Smith, John K., 2
sobriquets, *10*, 17, 29, 77, 103-104
society, 18-23, 57, 58, 61, 101, 104-105
Southern Pacific Railroad, 47, 48, 58, 71, 72, 73, 75, 77, 78, 95, 99, 101, 135, 136, 151
stablekeepers, *14*, 72, 73, 78, 99-100, 103, *112*
stage companies, 4, 26, 58, 98, 100
Sumner. *See* East Bakersfield.

tariffs, 47
Tehachapi, 135-137, *137-142*
Tehachapi Hotel, 136, *140, 141, 142*
Tehachapi Mountains, 4, 25, 26, 27, 45, 104, 135, 152
tinsmiths, 62
Toussaint, Antoine P., 62

Uhalt, Bernard, 103, *127*
Universal Hotel (East Bakersfield), 101, *119, 120*, 137
Utural, Jean, *51*

Vaca Valley Railroad, 98
Verdier, Eugène, 20, 26, *34*, 100-101
Verdier, Marie Laborde, 26, *34*, 101
Vial, Joe, 17, *83*
Vidaillet, Louis, 136

Vieux, Anaïs Villard Rostain, 75, *83, 86*
Vieux, André, 75, 77, *83*
Vieux, Joe, *49*
Vignave, Léopold, 26
Villard, Ambroise, 74, 75, *81, 82*
Villard, August, *14, 82*
Villard, Eugénie Faure, 74, *81, 82*
Villard, Pierre, 30
Villard, Rose Grimaud, 30
Villega, Francisco, 5
Vivian, Ambroise, *52*
Vivian, Célestin, *133*
Vivian, Germain, *123*
Vivian, Joseph (Jr.), *52*
Vivian, Lydie Eyraud, *133*

Wattier, Augustine, 53
Wattier, Léopold, 53, 54, 55
Weill, Alphonse, 58-59, 60, *64-65*
Weill, Henrietta Lévy, 59
Weill, Lawrence, 59
Weill Brothers' General Store (Bakersfield), *64, 65*
Wettel, Bob, 2
Weydenecht, Georges, 5
Wilson-Gorman Tariff, 47
World War I, xii-xiii, *14*, 21, 22, *43*, 48, 79
World War II, 22-23

Zampa, Jean, 101, 137, *141*
Zampa, Jennie Moynier Giraud, 136-*137*